# WICCA MAGIC

*Your Complete Guide to Wicca Herbal Magic and Wicca Spells That Will Fulfill Your Life*

## VIVIENNE GRANT

# CONTENTS

1. HISTORY AND ORIGIN OF THE WICCAN RELIGION     1
Gerald Gardner "Father of Wicca"     2

2. WICCAN PHILOSOPHY     11
The Wiccan Rede     13

3. SABBATS AND ESBATS     16
The Wheel Of The Year     17

4. THE SECRET TO WICCAN RITUALS     21

5. CREATING YOUR ALTAR     27

6. YOUR BOOK OF SHADOWS     31

7. ALL ABOUT HERBS     35
Herbs: A History     36

8. GARDENING TIPS AND GROWING YOUR OWN HERBS     40
Harvest, Dry and Store Your Herbs     45

9. DANGEROUS HERBS TO KEEP AWAY FROM     53

10. A GUIDE TO SUCCESSFUL SPELLCASTING     87
List of Spells to Try     99

Afterword     127

11. BIBLIOGRAPHY     128

# CHAPTER 1
## HISTORY AND ORIGIN OF THE WICCAN RELIGION

Wicca is referred to by many as the "Old Religion." Much of modern television and books draw inspiration from the Witch Trials of the 13th century, but in truth, the Wiccan religion is not really that old. Although it is believed that the rituals and practices were hidden from the Christian Church during the dark ages, in which the life of a Pagan would most certainly end in death, it was safe enough to surface in more modern times. This belief is what originally drew most to the religion and practices of Wicca.

In reality, Wicca is not an old religion at all. It first arrived in the United Kingdom in the mid-20th century around the 1940s or 1950s. Although, many of the things that influenced the religion are much older in comparison.

To become a Wiccan, one must be able to put themselves in the boots of those before them. To truly understand the laws, beliefs and traditions that come with the life of a Wiccan, you must have the knowledge of all of its origins.

The most important thing in a Wiccan's pursuit for a deeper connection and better understanding of Nature – and all its divine mystery – is the willingness to learn about the history behind that need.

Wiccans believe that nature is superior to them and not the other way around. The Wiccan Religion is a very free one despite its secretive and traditional routes. Most who chose to join the religion are not forced to follow one set of beliefs or traditions but instead has the freedom to believe in whatever they want and follow whichever traditions they feel are right for them.

The Wiccan Religion is truly the only one of its kind. It is magical in its own way as it allows each of its followers the freedom to seek out the natural magic of the earth and the magic within themselves in their own way.

## GERALD GARDNER "FATHER OF WICCA"

Gerald Gardner was born in England in 1884; he was a civil servant, author, and occultist. He traveled a lot in his youth and was interested in many things including anthropology, folklore, spiritualism and other occult beliefs. He is responsible for the birth of the modern Wiccan religion. He was part of a Rosicrucian Order that he joined in 1939, where he met friends who were part of a secret inner circle. They revealed to Gardner the truth of a coven of witches which he was initiated into that year.

In the 1920s, there was a theory of an ancient pagan religion that was still being practiced in secret throughout Western Europe. Margaret Murray, an anthropologist, called the religion a "Witch-cult." Gardner wanted to ensure the survival of the Witch-cult in the 20th century.

During the 1940s, Gardner founded a coven of his own and he named it Bricket Wood. He drew inspiration from a group he met called the New Forest group and when he created a new incarnation of the ancient Witch-cult, he borrowed much from their practices, including their elements of Freemasonry and their ceremonial magic.

Gardner was also responsible for the development of a major element in the Wicca practice: the worship of both a Goddess and a God. Both of which were equal to each other in every way.

The Wicca Religion although founded by Gerald Gardner was never called that by the man himself. He referred to the members of his coven as "the Wica," an Old English term for sorcerers. However, he always referred to the tradition itself as Witchcraft or just "the Craft." It only became known as Wicca after it spread to the United States.

Gerald Gardner is recognized as the father of modern Witchcraft but he didn't do it all by himself. His friends and colleagues were a part of it, as were other occultists. The inspiration that Gardner and other occultists were drawn from many older groups. Their knowledge, practices and rituals can be dated back to as early as the 13th century or the British occult revival in the 19th century. And of course those groups borrowed material from ancient civilizations before them.

So in modern times as we borrow our rituals and beliefs from our ancestors and their ancestors, it is an important part of the Wiccan religion that we remember its roots. For its roots within us is where the true magic comes from. The eternal, divine spirit that connects us to the earth and all its natural power has survived throughout the ages, no matter what stood in its path, to fulfil a divine purpose. Whether you believe it or not, for those who practice Wicca, or wish to practice Wicca, your experience will be based on how willing you are to lose yourself in the wonderful traditions of the "Old Religion."

· · ·

## Wicca Traditions and its Many Different Forms:

### Gardnerian Wicca

Gerald Gardner founded a coven which he called Bricket Wood, which is believed to have survived even today. This is an initiatory tradition, meaning that you can only be initiated into the group by another Gardnerian witch. This is so every Gardnerian can trace their lineage to the original Bricket Wood coven.

Gardnerian Wiccans work in covens that consist of 13 members. The coven is traditionally led by a High Priestess and a High Priest as second in command. This mirrors the story of the Sabbats, where the God dies and is reborn while the Goddess is eternal.

Their deities are the Mother Goddess and the Horned God, their specific names are kept secret from non-initiates. They traditionally used the Book of Shadows that was created by Gardner himself, for their rituals. Gardnerian rituals are elaborate and traditionally involved ritual sex. Whether or not this still occurs in modern day covens is unclear.

There are three separate degrees of initiation into the Gardnerian Wicca coven. This is probably borrowed from secret societies like the Freemasons. Gardnerian Wicca is one of the most secretive covens in existence, which makes it difficult for newcomers to learn the tradition.

### Alexandrian Wicca

Alexandrian Wicca is named not only after its founder Alex Sanders but also after the ancient Library of Alexandria. It was said to hold a great wealth of occult knowledge. Alex

Sanders and his wife Maxine were members of the Gardnerian Wicca after being initiated into one of the covens in early 1960.

Alexandrian Wicca shares similar traditions with Gardnerian Wicca. They also have three degrees of initiation, their covens are led by a High Priestess, and their belief in the supreme Goddess and a God remains the same. However they worship additional deities; the Oak King and Holly King. This is the ritual observation of the Wheel of the Year and the aspects of the God.

The Oak King and Holly King represent the changing of seasons as the two figures take turns ruling over the year. The Oak King takes reign throughout Spring and Summer, which are considered the light half of the year. The Holly King, however, reigns over the dark half which is Autumn and Winter.

Unlike the Gardnerian Wicca, the Alexandrian Wicca have the choice to practice in clothing rather than in the nude. The Alexandrian practice isn't as secretive as the Gardnerian. Although they do still respect their traditions, there is an allowance for growth and following your own path. This allows for changes and adjustments as the Alexandrian Wicca practitioners see fit.

**Dianic Wicca**

Dianic Wicca originated in the United States and it is different from the old traditions. It is a feminist tradition that worships the Goddess solely and celebrates her supremacy; unlike the Gardnerian Wicca that focuses on the balance between both the God and the Goddess.

The original Dianic tradition was founded by Zsuzsanna Budapest in the 1970s. Those initiated through Budapest's lineage are female-only. Although there was a form of the Dianic Wiccan practice formed later by Morgan McFarland and Mark Roberts, that admit men into their covens as well. There are also other traditions also inspired by the Dianic Wicca who also admits men as well as women into their coven.

In Dianic covens, there is more spiritual growth and freedom allowed within the coven. They meet on Esbats, Sabbats, and significant times when someone in the community is in need. They have a very fluid and woman-centered approach in their circles.

## Seax-Wicca

Seax-Wicca was formed in the United States by Raymond Buckland in 1970. He was a High Priest in the Gardnerian Tradition and brought the religion with him to New York in 1960. He founded Seax-Wicca so he could continue the practice of Gardnerianism but in a way that was suitable for Americans.

He was inspired by the Anglo-Saxon Witchcraft which was practiced between the $5^{th}$ and $11^{th}$ centuries. Their deities are called Woden and Freya, they represent the God and Goddess. They study herbal lore and forms of divination, which include Tarot and runes.

The Seax-Wiccans lack secrecy. The coven members have no oath that they take so it is easy to find out about their rituals and traditions. Their rituals and celebrations are open to outsiders and newcomers if they choose it to be. They welcome new ideas, magic and rituals into their practices as there isn't Book of Shadows tradition for them to follow.

Coven leaders are elected democratically and they serve a term of one lunar year which is the equivalent of 13 full moons. Being initiated by another Seax-Wicca witch isn't needed as self-dedication is acceptable as an entry to this form of the Craft.

### Eclectic Wicca

Eclectic Wicca is not exactly a "tradition" by any standards as the only thing each practitioner has in common is that they're different from any other coven or form of the Wiccan practice.

Eclectic Wicca is similar to the practice of Solitary Wicca however, there are several covens and groups that also fit this category. The only actual tradition they have is the desire to walk their own path and be as unique as they can.

Each individual Eclectic Wiccan "invents" their own form of religion, ritual, or beliefs. Some borrow from two or more of existing forms of the religion while others create their own form of the religion from their imagination. In fact, some of the Eclectic Wicca practitioners would not even agree with the term "religion."

The creation of the eclectic practice comes from many different reasons, but it's often solitary Wiccans that have no community for them to learn from.

### Solitary Wicca

Solitary Wicca is the practice of Wicca by individuals by themselves rather than forming part of a coven and practicing in a group. Most newcomers to the Wiccan religion start as solitaires learning through books or from others. They may even create their own practices, taking from many other traditions and choosing their own beliefs and deities to worship.

There are some members of covens who later choose to move to solitary practice for several reasons. It doesn't matter if you practice in a large, open coven, a small, secretive coven, or if you choose solitary practice. The essence of the religion lay in the beliefs, rituals and traditions that get carried out no matter what form of Wicca you choose.

## Choosing The Right Path

The Wiccan Tradition can be dated back to ancient times, but from the first instances of Witchcraft and Magic showing up in the history books to the very first coven ever created, it remains the same. The tradition may change depending on which coven you choose to follow or which form of the religion you choose to believe in. In the end, it doesn't matter which rituals or traditions you follow or which Gods you want to believe in. The only thing that matters in the end is the magic you feel around you.

All these choices might seem daunting to newcomers or outsiders, but you don't have to choose now. That's why Solitary Wiccans exist; you don't need to choose a coven or tradition to follow in order to be a practitioner.

You can take as much time as you need and learn at your own pace. If you want to make sure that you make the right choice that is completely and undeniably right for you then you need to take your time. The choice between the different forms of Wiccan tradition and religion is not a choice that should be made lightly. However, you don't have to worry if you do end up making the wrong choice, you can change your mind whenever you want.

If you choose to follow the Dianic Wicca tradition but later on decide that you prefer the practices of the Gardnerian Wicca then you have the choice to change at any time. Although once you get into the different forms of rituals and deities to worship, the change will not be easy but it is still an available option.

So my advice to all newcomers to the Wiccan Religion is to take all the time you need. Learn as much as you can from as many sources as you can. Take information and knowledge from every kind of place you can think of, this includes books, movies, T.V. series and online sources. There is no such thing as being overprepared.

Here is a list of recommended movies to watch, the creators of which have managed to follow the different forms of each Wicca practice very well;

- Practical Magic (released in 1998)
- The Covenant (released in 2006)
- The Witch (released in 2016)
- Beautiful Creatures (released in 2013)
- American Horror Story: Coven, Season Three (released in 2013)
- The Craft (released in 1996)

As you can see from the list of movies, from the ones released in the 1990s to the more modern ones that the Wiccan Religion is no longer hidden or frowned upon. It once was during the dark ages and the Witch Trials but now it is a more acceptable and widely spread religion. So if you are new to the religion and have any fear of being ridiculed or isolated then put those fears to rest. There are many practitioners and followers out there that the only way you'll ever feel alone is if you want to be.

After you're done and you believe you are ready to truly choose your path, the only other bit of advice I can give is this: follow your heart. The divine natural magic of the earth lives inside all of us and when it comes time to choose your path then I can promise you that your heart will never lead you astray. Listen to it carefully and never take it for granted.

However, as mentioned before, you don't need to choose to be part of the Wiccan Religion. Your belief in the Gods and your dedication to the practice is all you need to be a true Wiccan.

# CHAPTER 2
## WICCAN PHILOSOPHY

Wiccan Philosophy is a difficult subject to discuss whether you practice the religion or not. Especially with all the different traditions that have branched out of the original Gardnerian Wicca. Although all forms of the Wiccan religion came from some other forms of tradition, even the original coven created by Gerald Gardner, all of them share a similar philosophy.

Even though there are many different forms of Wiccan traditions and followings, the overall philosophy of the religion has remained the same, or at least similar.

The Divine:

One philosophy that remains the same in any form of the religion is the deities. The different adaptions of the Wiccan traditions have a larger list of deities but the basic philosophy surrounds the Goddess and the God. As the male and female can be seen in all of nature and so it is reflected by the Divine Goddess and the Horned God.

·  ·  ·

Nature is Sacred:

Every Wiccan's goal, no matter what coven they are a part of or which tradition they follow, the bound with nature itself remains strong. To work side by side with nature as it is an extension of the Goddess and God themselves. The natural cycles are celebrated; this includes both seasonal cycles as well as cycles such as the cycle of life and death. These times of celebration are also times of rituals and spellcasting as the cycle of nature is believed to heighten a Wiccan's inner power and energy.

Magick:

The belief in magick and how it surrounds us and all we do is a big part of the Wiccan philosophy. Although not all who follow the traditions and practices of the Wiccan religion take part in any form of spell work. Even if they do not participate in spells or rituals, they still believe in the existence and importance of magick in everyday life.

Faith is on a Personal Level:

Wiccans, whether they are in a coven or working solitary, connect to the Goddess and God personally. It is believed that you are responsible for maintaining and building upon that personal relationship with the deities all on your own. You connect with the Goddess and the God on a personal level and it is only up to you as to how close you become with them. Not even the other members of your coven can be considered responsible for that relationship as they too are working on their own personal connection to the deities.

No Path is the Wrong Path:

Wiccans do not believe that their religion is the only valid one. They believe that any path that leads to the Divine is an acceptable path to take. There are many religions who believe that theirs is the only path to take - this is not the case with Wiccans. No path is the wrong path; if you are able to find your way to the Divine then you are on the right path.

## THE WICCAN REDE

Among the things you will learn when choosing the path you will take to Wiccan practices is one of the main principles that all Wiccans follow. It is referred to as the only 'rule' in Wicca;

**"An' It Harm None, Do What Ye Will."**

The main takeaway from this is to avoid harming anyone or anything. Wicca is a religion centered on Earth, life and working alongside nature itself, so adopting this concept as one of their main principles makes sense. This rule is known as the Wiccan Rede.

This policy of doing no harm is the reason that Wiccans end their spells with phrases such as "with harm to none," and other similar forms of wordings. The way the Wiccan Rede is worded can be attributed to Doreen Valiente, who was the author for much of Gerald Gardner's ritual material for his Bricket Wood Coven. The Wiccan Rede is a line in a speech by Doreen Valiente that was recorded in mid-1960s. Although it's pseudo-archaic language makes it difficult for newcomers to understand the policy it comes with, it is easy to understand by anyone. It can be translated into a more informal state which makes it easier to read; "If it doesn't hurt anyone, then do whatever you want."

A statement made by Aleister Crowley is believed to be the inspiration for the Wiccan Rede. He applied this statement to his own religion, Thelema, which was: "Do what thou wilt shall be the whole of the Law."

Crowley is believed to have made a huge impression on Gerald Gardner during their time as friends. He drew much inspiration from Crowley's religion when he was creating his own version of the Wiccan religion. Whatever turns out to be the true inspiration for the Wiccan Rede, it is a widely-known hallmark and tradition of the Wiccan Philosophy.

**Is The Wiccan Rede a Rule?**

Most Wiccans and newcomers to the religion are confused by the Wiccan Rede. It is stated as being a rule but there are no actual guidelines or official authoritative to follow. So is the Wiccan Rede an actual rule or is it just a guideline or a form of advice to follow? There is no answer to this question unfortunately but there is some evidence we can go by for our own answer.

The word Rede means 'advice' or 'counsel,' so by those descriptions we can say that the word Rede is more of a guideline than a rule. Although the Wiccan religion is about taking responsibility for your actions, so "harm none" is the advice that many Wiccans follow. So all who practice the religion believe that they can do whatever they wish as long as it sends no harm or negative energy to anyone around them.

*The Rule of Three*

The Rule of Three also known as Three-fold Law or Law of Return, is a religious tenet that almost all Wiccans, Pagans, or Occultists follow. This law states that all energy someone puts out into the world, whether it is negative energy or positive energy, will be returned to that person three times or three-fold.

The Rule of Three is also described as karma by some Wiccans, as both concepts explain the prospect of cause to effect and encourages its followers to act in an appropriate way. Those who follow The Rule of Three are more likely to only send positive energy out into the world so that they will only receive positive energy in return rather than sending out negative energy and receiving it back threefold.

The Rule of Three first appeared in Gerald Gardner's 1949 novel 'High Magic's Aid':

**"Thou hast obeyed the Law. But mark well, when thou receivest good, so equally art bound to return good three-fold." (For this is the joke in witchcraft, the witch knows, though the initiate does not, that she will get three times what she gave, so she does not strike hard.)**

This brings light to the belief that all who wishes to follow the practices of Wiccan Religion do no harm to others as The Rule of Three states that it will only bring more harm to their self. This is also the reason that most if not all Wiccans are pacifists.

# CHAPTER 3
## SABBATS AND ESBATS

A Sabbat is a holiday or celebration surrounding a certain natural event as one season changes into another. These holidays are usually some of the only times you'll see an entire coven gathered together, aside from other events like an Esbat.

An Esbat is different from a Sabbat where it's not a holiday or even a celebration to most; however, it is still regarded with the same amount of importance. During an Esbat is one of the other times a coven will gather and partake in rituals, dances and other events. The Esbats are the celebration of the 13 full moons that there are in the year.

The Sabbats and Esbats are said to be some of the most naturally powerful times of the year. It is recommended that rituals and spells that require a lot of energy be performed during one of these celebrations. All forms of magick rely on energy, both from nature and from the Wiccan themselves. These particular days are best known for heightening not only the energy of nature but also the energy within a Wiccan. This is why most covens will gather on these days and perform group rituals or spells, because not only are their personal powers strengthened, the power of the earth around them is also much stronger.

THE WHEEL OF THE YEAR

Yule: Winter Solstice

**Around December 21st**

This is the time of the year where the night length is at its peak. At Yule, it is the shortest day of the year and the longest night of the year. From this day, the sunlight returns as the days lengthen. Yule is the celebration of the rebirth of the Sun God. This celebration has been around for centuries and some of the Christmas traditions were adopted from the traditions of the Wiccan holiday. The date of Yule changes from the 20th to the 22nd each year.

Traditions include: gift giving, lighting a Yule log, and decorating a tree indoors.

Imbolc: Brigid's Day

**February 2nd**

Imbolc is dedicated to the Celtic Goddess Brigid but it is also a celebration for the first signs of spring. This is also a holiday for non-Wiccans known as Groundhog Day. This is a time to make a new start in life and change things up a little bit; most Wiccans start by spring cleaning their home.

Traditions include: making a bed for Brigid, cleaning as mentioned before, and sometimes burning fires.

Ostara: Spring Equinox

**Around March 21st**

This is an equinox, which means the day and the night are the same lengths. This is a day to celebrate new life and new beginnings. Eggs and bunnies are symbols that are traditionally used to represent this day. It is yet another Wiccan holiday that has been borrowed to make the non-Wiccan holiday known as Easter.

Just as Yule, the date of Ostara changes from the 20th to the 22nd. On this day, it is suggested that you plant seeds of goals and the extra energy given from nature this day will give you a better chance at success.

Traditions include: decorating with spring flowers, coloring with eggs or cooking with eggs.

Beltane: Walpurgis Night

## May 1st

The Sun God that was reborn during Yule is a man now and this is the time of year for the sacred union between God and Goddess. Beltane is a time to celebrate fertility, love, sexuality, and growth. Celebrate it with joy however you choose to.

Traditions include: Lighting bonfires outdoors and dancing around a ribbon wrapped May Pole.

Litha: Summer Solstice

## Around June 21st

This is the other solstice on the calendar and it is the longest day of the year. Just like Yule and Ostara, this holiday usually occurs on the 21st but it may vary. On this day, the Sun God starts to lose his strength as the days shorten in length. On this day, the Goddess has left her Maiden form from Imbolc and is now entering her Mothering aspect.

Traditions for this day include the collecting of herbs.

Lammas:

**August 1st**

Lammas revolves around the harvesting of grains and baking bread. It is the first of the three harvest festivals there are in the year. It was common to make sacrifices to ensure a good harvest over the next two harvest festivals.

Traditions include: making cornhusk dollies and baking bread.

Mabon: Autumn Equinox

**Around September 21st**

This is the second harvest festival and the day and night have become equal again on the equinox. The weather grows cold around this holiday as the winter approaches. It was consid ered a tradition on this holiday to have rituals in which you give thanks which have been borrowed for another non-Wiccan holiday, Thanksgiving.

Traditions include: Rituals of thanks, giving to the poor, and the making and drinking of wine.

Samhain: All Hallows

**Oct 31st**

This is the last harvest festival and it marks the end of the Wiccan year. The God has died and will be mourned by the Goddess until Yule when he is reborn once again. Samhain is yet another Sabbat that is celebrated as a non-Wiccan holiday called Halloween. Wiccans do not give out candy or go from door to door collecting it though. This time of the year for Wiccans is a darker time as it is a time for the dead.

Traditions include: remembering the dead, divination, and carving Jack o' Lanterns.

Being a Wiccan doesn't mean that you are obligated to celebrate these holidays, nor are you expected not to celebrate other holidays such as Christmas or Easter. To join in these celebrations and beliefs of what these days represent is a completely personal choice. Just like Wiccans believe that all paths that lead to the Divine are the right path, they also believe in the right to practice the religion how you want to.

Knowing and understanding these traditions and beliefs surrounding these holidays might help you get closer to your own energy. These holidays revolve around a time of year where a nature cycle changes and starts anew, as if a part of nature is dying and a new part is being reborn every year.

The God dies and is reborn every year while the Goddess remains eternal, this reflects the changing seasons and the Earth itself. Understanding how this works can help you get closer to nature as a Wiccan and as a person and it will most certainly give you more success in your spell casting.

# CHAPTER 4

# THE SECRET TO WICCAN RITUALS

Rituals are the core elements of the Wiccan religion. They are the center of every celebration, including Sabbats and Esbats. Wicca is a loosely structured spiritual tradition which is part of what draws most newcomers to the religion. However, no matter which traditions you follow or which coven you choose to be part of, there is one core element that remains the same: a Wiccan ritual.

Covens will gather to worship the Goddess and God and celebrate the cycles of life. Even a Solitary Wiccan will participate in a ritual and add their own personal energy into the collection of magical energy that everyone will be releasing into the air on these occasions. A solo ritual is just as important and significant as a ritual performed by a larger group or coven.

Wiccan rituals are usually held in private although some covens will hold their rituals in public. This allows for outsiders to observe if they are interested and perhaps learn more about the religion as it is usually stereotyped. There are some Wiccan covens that will even invite members of the public to participate in the ritual if they are willing.

• • •

## The Basics

A Wiccan ritual should make you feel comfortable, at one with nature and personally connected to the Goddess and God themselves. It is a beautiful and elegant celebration of the ever changing cycle of nature and it is nothing if not mysterious.

There are many types of rituals and no two will look alike. Each Sabbat and Esbat calls for a different celebration, which means a different ritual needs to be performed. The difference in between rituals also lies in the Wiccan or coven that is performing it. Some rituals will be tightly structured and extremely elaborate; this is usually only the case with certain covens. Since most covens keep to themselves and their secrets are only known to members, it's difficult to accurately know what their rituals consist of.

Rituals usually practiced by solitary Wiccans or even small groups of them are more likely to be simpler. Some Wiccans are more creative and design their rituals while they are performing them. In the end, the main content of any ritual is based on the occasion it is being used to celebrate.

There is a clear difference between the Sabbats and the Esbats; the Esbats are a celebration of the 13 full moons that take part throughout the year; these rituals will be focused on the Goddess as she is the embodiment of the Moon itself. Sabbats however are year round holidays that are scheduled around the yearly cycle of nature and its transformation through the seasons. These are celebrations of the relationship between the Goddess and the God. Each Sabbat is either a celebration of their birth, transformation, unison, death, and rebirth.

As mentioned earlier in this book, there are many different forms of the Wiccan religion and the beliefs in the deities but the basics of your rituals will usually remain prominent.

• • •

## Purification

The first step will always be the purification of the body of the Wiccan and of the place where the ritual will be performed. Purification is necessary to rid the body, mind, and space of all negative energy it may be carrying. This happens in two forms.

A Wiccan can perform a ritual bath to rid them of any unwanted energies. This is not just to cleanse the body but also the mind and the soul. You can use it as a time to reflect on things, perhaps things you want to be washed away during the bath. Anything from a bad habit to even a bad thought you had during the day.

For the Purification of a ritual space, you can use a smudging ceremony to cleanse the area. Smudging involves burning sacred herbs so the smoke can drown out all the negative energy. The most traditional herbs used in a smudging ritual are sage, lavender, and rosemary.

## Setting up an Altar

You'll need to set up an Altar next. Some Wiccans have a permanent Altar in their homes or place of worship. Even if there is a permanent Altar set up, you'll find that the decorations will need to change depending on the occasion that will be celebrated. Other than that, the Altar is arranged with Wiccan tools, offerings, and symbols. These will need to be laid out accordingly as each of the various traditions has a certain way to lay out their Altar.

For large rituals performed by members of a coven, the Altar tends to be much larger than your usual household Altar.

## Casting the Circle

The Casting of the Circle is an act Wiccans use to create a boundary between the sacred space they've created and the mundane world outside. This circle is meant to be drawn around the Altar, with the Altar situated directly in the middle but with plenty of room around it for all who will be taking part in the ritual. They must be able to move around freely within the circle and there must be no chance of stepping out of the boundary or bumping into one another.

The circle is traditionally marked with a long cord which is used to trace the circle, sea salt, herbs, several stones, or candles. This is only one method for casting a circle but this is the simplest way for beginners.

**Begin the Ritual**

After the circle has been cast then the ritual can begin. The order in which things are performed may vary depending on traditions and depending on the Wiccan's choices. What usually occurs first is the God and Goddess is invited into the circle to join the ritual. Then the four classical elements are invoked, being Earth, Water, Fire, and Air. These are the materials that make up the very existence of everything so any ritual done without them is a ritual poor of magical energy. In some Wiccan traditions, there is a fifth element that is also called to the ritual; the fifth element is traditionally known as Spirit.

Other traditions replace this step with something called Calling the Quarters; instead of the four elements or in addition to them the four directions are called. North, East, South, and West will also add their own form of magical energy to the circle when they are invited.

Once you have completed these steps then you can dive straight into the heart of the ritual. The intent of the occasion must be stated, as in whether you are here to celebrate a Sabbat, Esbat, or any other occasion. When rituals are performed for a reason other than the celebration of a Wiccan holiday, they are usually done separately. This allows for any celebration involving the worship of the Goddess and God to be completely focused on the deities during the ritual.

After you have stated the intent of the ritual then the main body can begin; this can consist of many different activities. The main activity of any ritual, depending on the tradition being followed, is the reenactment of a scene or scenes from myths or poems from ancient times. The kind of material used in this drama reenactment will solely depend on the traditions of the Wiccan group that are being followed during this ritual. Solitary Wiccans might also reenact their own myths or poems that they adhere to in their own traditions; some may even write their own poetry for the occasion and recite it.

Other events of the night will include ritual dancing and/or singing and/or chanting which is usually done as a group around the Altar. Other ritual gestures may be performed depending on the type of occasion. Most traditions set aside a time of reflection during the ritual, used to reflect on the blessings that have been received throughout the season. A Wiccan may offer prayers to the Goddess and God at this time if they wish to. These prayers can be personal or for the benefit of someone else or even for the bettering of an entire community. On some occasions, it is considered traditional to offer up prayers on behalf of an entire community or even the whole of humanity.

In many traditions, the ritual usually comes to an end with a ceremony known as "cakes and wine," this ceremony is used to close a ritual but it can and has been used to start a ritual with. During this ceremony, food and drink are offered to all participants and is symbolically shared between them and the

Goddess and God. The ceremony is supposed to draw a connection between the spiritual plane and Earth, which helps to center everyone who was involved in the ritual before they close the ritual proceedings.

Once the "cake and wine" ceremony is complete then the Elements, the Goddess, the God, and all who were called to join, are formally thanked and are released from the circled. Then the circle is closed, marking that the ritual has come to an end.

These are just the basic workings of a typical ritual that a Solitary Wiccan, or Wiccan coven will perform. You may become a member of a coven and they could possibly have their own traditions and rituals that must be followed. It's likely that most covens follow a tradition of their own that is either sort of similar to these basics or are completely different. If you have chosen to take your own path as a Solitary Wiccan then you are more than welcome to create your own rituals and practices to follow. As long as your intentions for the God and Goddess are sincere and you can remain focused on the actions you are performing and the reason you are there, then it is perfectly acceptable.

Remember that any path that leads to the Divine can never be the wrong path.

# CHAPTER 5

# CREATING YOUR ALTAR

What is an Altar and why do you need one? Well, you don't need one. It isn't required of any Wiccan tradition to have a dedicated space where you perform your rituals or cast your spells. It's customary for a Wiccan to have a personal space where they can work and focus their energy but not every Wiccan has one.

An Altar is a safe space a Wiccan can go to that is their own. It's a place where one can perform their magick in peace and having a workspace can only help better your focus on your work. It is a sacred place where you can keep all your magickal supplies and escape to for some solitude with your natural energy.

If you feel you have no need for an Altar then that is no problem as it isn't a necessary thing to have. However, you may feel you want one later in your journey to the Divine. Here are a few tips to help you on your way to creating your own Altar.

**Where should it go?**

Wherever you want to put it. As mentioned, a Wiccan's Altar is a sacred place, where one can feel comfortable and relaxed. You must be able to lose yourself in the energy within you and the energy around you, so placing your Altar somewhere that makes you feel comfortable and safe is a good start.

It can be out in the open, perhaps in a greenhouse amongst nature and the herbs you grow. If you don't have a green-house, then perhaps placing it in the garden or on the front porch will be good enough. Getting closer to nature will heighten your connection to the deities as well as your energy but if you don't feel comfortable having your Altar outside then it will hinder you more than help you.

A quiet, more personal space is also an option if it will make you feel more comfortable. Much like a study, you can have a small, private room dedicated to your Altar instead. Some-where that allows you to close the door and draw the curtains for a more private and personal experience. There is nothing wrong with wanting to keep your Altar to yourself. A Wiccan's Altar is their space to be comfortable.

You can have your Altar anywhere in your home. If you're the type of Wiccan that works a lot with herbs and tea, which means you spend a lot of time in the kitchen,. then you can place your Altar in your kitchen. The same goes if you spend a lot of time in your living area, then you can place your Altar there. The only thing you need to remember when looking for a place to put your Altar is that you need to feel comfortable with yourself and the things around you. That is the purpose of an Altar

## Hidden Altars

Sometimes you may need to keep your Altar a secret from others. Not everyone is completely acceptable to the beliefs and traditions of others; this is the same with Wiccans. There may be some members of your family or some of your friends that aren't acceptable of the way of life that you have chosen. With any hope, you will never have to come up against these circumstances, however, it does still happen.

You may need to hide your belief in the Wiccan religion from people around you who don't accept it but that doesn't mean you have to forgo the whole experience. If you still want to have an Altar but are unable to keep it out where there is a chance of it being discovered then there are several options.

A temporary Altar is one of the easiest and more accessible options. You can just keep all the things you have that make up an Altar in a box. You can keep the box under your bed, in your cupboard; anywhere you think it will remain hidden. Whenever you need to use it, say for a spell or a ritual, then simply take the box out and unpack all your things. A nice cloth can turn any ordinary flat surface into a functioning Altar. When you're finished, simply pack your Altar back into its box and put it back in its hiding place.

Another valid option, although a tad more difficult to perform, is to hide your Altar in plain sight. You don't need to create an Altar that looks extremely traditional or has brooms, candles and cauldrons on it, like it is in the movies. Those things are used to make up an Altar but if you need to hide yours then you can use less noticeable objects. All you need is a little bit of creativity and you can have your fully functional Altar in plain sight if you're careful about it.

**What Makes an Altar?**

As with the location of the Altar, what you keep on it is completely up to you. There are of course several traditional objects and tools that many place on their Altars. For instance, many like to represent the elements with objects on their Altar, this is a must if you wish to form a stronger connection with nature. Things you can use that represent the elements:

- For Water, you can use a goblet or chalice, or perhaps a glass of water or seashells
- For Earth, a few stones, or a bowl filled with earth or salt (a Pentacle is traditionally used to represent Earth)
- For fire, some candles, or incense, or something colored red (like a stone or crystal)
- Feathers can be used to represent Air

There are some other traditional items to place on your Altar but not all of them are necessary, as mentioned, it is up to you entirely. If you work with a specific type of spell work, such as candles or herbs, then keeping those objects on your Altar is acceptable. This is your personal space so whatever you say goes. However, here is a list of some common items if you want to go the traditional way:

- A statuary representing the Deities
- A Wand
- A Cauldron
- Candles
- Bells
- A ritual knife
- Plants
- Crystals
- Feathers

So when choosing a spot to put your Altar and when you're deciding what objects to keep on it, just keep these few things in mind. This is your space, your opinion is the only one that matters. If it harms none, do what you will.

## CHAPTER 6
## YOUR BOOK OF SHADOWS

A Book of Shadows or a "grimoire" is a confusing item for many newcomers and people just starting their journey into Wicca. There are a lot of rumors and fantasies made up about it, such as a Book of Shadows being a sacred object passed down from generation to generation and that it is the only source of true magick. Stories like this are accredited to modern movies and television.

The truth is that there isn't a single Book of Shadows that is kept secret from outsiders and untrusted newcomers; there only used to be. When Gerald Gardner first formed his coven, they had a shared Book of Shadows that was kept secret from anyone who was not an initiated member. However, these are ancient practices and it is far more common nowadays for each Wiccan to have their own personal Book of Shadows.

Now if you're new to the Wiccan religion then you should keep in mind that keeping a Book of Shadows is not necessary and you can avoid the process altogether. However, if you are interested, making your own Book of Shadows is a rewarding experience and it will become a very important tool in all of your rituals and spell castings.

. . .

**What is a Book of Shadows?**

A Wiccan's Book of Shadows is a very personal tool that is for their eyes only, or for whomever they trust enough to show. Think of it as a journal or a diary, you can use it to record how well a spell went or you can write about a magickal or spiritual experience you had. Your Book of Shadows is yours alone, so it can contain whatever you want it to but it usually contains information solely about your Wiccan beliefs, rituals, etc.

Many people also use their Book of Shadows as a kind of recipe book or a guide. You can write down rituals you want to perform or that you have performed so you forget the specific steps that need to be taken. Or you can write a list of spells or recipes for herbal magick and potions. No one expects you to keep this knowledge in your head and be able to remember all of it off by heart.

Some Wiccans prefer to call their book a Book of Light, or just shorten it to B.o.S, its ancient name is a grimoire but that isn't an easy word to slip into a conversation. You won't always be free to speak about your Wiccan beliefs with others, as mentioned before, not everyone is accepting of the religion. However if you do wish to speak about it, let's say with a friend at their house but you don't want their roommate to hear then simply use whatever name you've decided to give your book. This is a personal Wiccan item and whatever happens to it is your choice.

As for what you should use as your Book of Shadows, well that too is up to you. Although, most would like to write with black ink and a quill in a leather bound book, with yellow stained pages and a big metal lock keeping it closed shut. You may have seen books like this in the movies and although it would be a cool addition to your Altar, it's not really necessary.

You can have a normal exam book, a notepad or you can even go digital and keep your Book of Shadows on your laptop or phone. However, I don't recommend this as you may be working around liquids in the future, whether it is for a spell or other magickal creations, and you don't want to risk damaging your device.

Most Wiccans who have been working on their own Book of Shadows over years of practice would recommend a book that allows you to remove and add pages easily. A ringed binder isn't the most mystical looking book but it is perfect for the job. At the end of the day when choosing your book, you should think practical rather than something that fits the mood or looks "witchy."

With a ringed binder, pages can be removed, added and moved around without damaging the book or the pages. A ringed binder also allows for the addition of dividers so you can easily organize your Book of Shadows. You can separate the herbal magick recipes from the spells and you can separate the Esbat rituals from the Sabbat rituals. It might not be the best looking addition to your Altar but it is practical and it gets the job done. It's definitely a good place to start.

Remember when choosing what to put in your Book of Shadows, it is your personal tool to help with your Wiccan practices. There is no right or wrong way to make one, there is only the way that suits you best.

As for any tool in a Wiccan's use, your Book of Shadows must be blessed. This can be done in a simple ritual, which I have already elaborated on earlier. You must follow all the steps of a usual ritual:

- Cleanse the ritual area of negative energy

- Cast the circle around your Altar
- Call the Deities, invoke the Elements, or call the Quarters (you can do more than one of these)
- Bless your Book of Shadows

Your blessing can be a simple incantation that you write yourself, something as simple as "I bless this Book of Shadows in the presence of the God and Goddess," or "May the God and Goddess bless my book and protect it from all negative energy."

When doing the blessing ritual, keep in mind the Wiccan Rede and the Rule of Three, if you do not abide by these, then the blessing on your Book of Shadows may backfire.

- Complete the ritual how you usually would

Thank the Deities and everything else you invoked or called into your circle, open the circle you drew and ground yourself.

Your Book of Shadows is now blessed and you can start adding your rituals and writing your own spells, or adding other spells that you've used.

# CHAPTER 7
## ALL ABOUT HERBS

The Wiccan practice and all of the rituals and traditions involved require working side by side with nature itself. Nature does not work for you and you do not work for nature. You must learn to see and treat it as your equal. This bind you form with nature is precisely why Herbal magic is some of the most powerful magic you could learn.

The simple fact that working with herbs is working with nature directly and all of the magic from the Earth itself is the reason herbal magic is so powerful. The existence of herbs outdates humans by centuries, and they had all that time alone with the Earth to soak up all of its natural magic.

You may ask, what exactly is an herb? Well, there are scientists, biologists, cooks and even gardeners that will tell you all the specifics that constitute the category of herbs. To a Wiccan, an herb can range from a flower, to a tree, to a shrub, or even a weed. Every creation of the Earth has magical properties which is why a Wiccan would choose to use it. Even dangerous and poisonous plants have their uses in Wiccan spells and rituals.

I bet at one point in your life you watched an old film, or even a recent one, where a group of witches (usually three) are gathering around a big, black cauldron bubbling over onto the floor. These witches throw all sorts of things into this cauldron while shouting out things like 'Eye of a Bat' or 'Toad's Tongue' and all kinds of things like that. Now I'm sure that might have been terrifying to a child but ridiculous and laughable to an adult, however, there is some truth and history behind such rituals.

In ancient times, those names were given to a certain part of a tree, flower, or any kind of ingredient that they were using at the time. This was a way to keep trade secrets of a coven so no outsiders or untrusted newcomers would be able to copy their many spells or traditions. Herbal magic is such a difficult magic to master that its secrets are still to this day closely guarded in some covens.

To master the practice of herbal magic could take years but it isn't an impossible task. There are a few simple things you can start with that make it easier and get you into the practice. The work might be hard but the rewards and benefits are well worth it in the end.

While working with herbs, just keep in mind that you are working alongside nature itself and that there is no act a Wiccan can perform that is greater than giving back to the Earth.

HERBS: A HISTORY

Since the first plant reached up out of the soil towards the sun and soaked up the energy it provided; the first plant to drink the water from the air and beneath the ground, allowed it to spread its roots deep and wide. The first time its seed was spread far and wide allowing even more plants to dig themselves into the soil of the Earth and provide the creatures that walk among them air, food, and energy.

A plant is the perfect role model for a Wiccan. It lives its life for the Earth and all the creatures living on it. A plant lives side by side with nature, taking only what it needs to survive and always giving back more than it has taken. This has been the way since the dawn of life. A true Wiccan can only hope to live his or her life the way a plant does.

Every plant has its own magical potential and magical properties. This hasn't changed in all the centuries that these plants have been on Earth. Thousands of years ago a plant would be used for its medical properties, whether those properties are to heal a wound or simply numb the pain of one. Today, that exact same plant will still carry the same magical potential.

If our ancestors used to boil a specific herb into a cup of tea, drink it and receive good health and luck then we can do the same thing with the same herb today. Our ancestors would study a plant and all the things it could provide. They would spend hours in the forests and in the green fields searching for and gathering up herbs they could use. They memorized every useful herb and all its magical and medical properties. Today, we can benefit from the knowledge and wisdom that our ancestors spent years accumulating. However, that does not mean that there is no longer something new to learn.

There will always be something new for us to learn. There is always something nature can teach us. As a Wiccan, you must be ready and open to learning anything anyone has to teach you. That is the only way we can grow and give back to the Earth.

## Connection Between Herbs and the Elements

Each stage of a plant's life is the embodiment of each one of the four classical Wiccan elements, Fire, Earth, Water, and Air, not including the fifth element known as Spirit. This connection to the elements is the reason plants offer so much power and magic to whoever knows how to use them.

Earth is the foundation of life. It is our home and provides us sustenance. It is versatile and always present, it is represented by many things around the planet, including the forests, caves, valleys, and gardens. Earth is associated with abundance, prosperity, and strength.

Air is crucial to our existence. It is all around us yet we never see it. It is represented by the wind, birds and the sky. Air is associated with the mind, intellect, divination and communication.

Fire is not necessary for human survival in modern times; however, we could not live without it for a brief period in history. Fire is the only one of the elements that cannot be touched by the human body without causing harm. It is represented by the Sun, stars, and volcanoes. Fire is the element of transformation. It is associated with illumination, creativity, strength, and health.

Water is thought to be the most essential element in sustaining life. Humans and other creatures of the Earth cannot live without it, including plants. It is considered to be a shape-shifter as it takes many forms but remains the same element. It is represented by rain, streams, lakes, and oceans. Water is associated with the Moon, dreams, psychic abilities, and the realm of emotions.

The first element each plant interacts with is Earth. A plant starts as a seed in the soil of the Earth where it finds all the nutrients and foods it requires to sustain itself. Next, the sunlight or Fire element gives the plant the energy it needs to grow further above the ground. Each plant has the need to reach up towards the fire of the sun that gives all things life. The Fire element directly interacts with the Air element as it starts the process of converting carbon dioxide, a poison to us but a form of food to plants, into fresh breathable air. The element of Air in turn carries more spores, or seed of the plant to new ground where more plants can grow and continue the process.

The final stage involves the element of Water. All living things need water to live; this includes all forms of plants. Even a cactus that grows in the desert where water is scarce still needs it to survive and grow. Not only does a plant need water to live, the water requires its help as well. Plants take up a crucial part of the Earth's water cycle as they purify it and move the water from within the soil into the atmosphere.

Once again, a plant not only takes what it needs from the four elements, it always gives back to the Earth more than it has taken. This is a practice all Wiccans perform when working with Herbal Magic.

## CHAPTER 8
## GARDENING TIPS AND GROWING YOUR OWN HERBS

The best form of Herbal Magic is when you grow the herbs you use yourself. This gets you closer to nature and allows you the opportunity to power the herbs with your own energy. This will give your rituals and spells a greater form of magic and the herbs will carry more power in them.

It's okay if you don't have the best gardening skills or a green thumb of any kind. Gardening is an art form but it can be taught to a Wiccan willing to learn.

Growing your own herbs is one of the best things you can do when working with Herbal Magic, but it isn't necessary. If you wish to skip the gardening process as it takes too long for your liking and you're eager to get to the spell casting and potion making side of things, that is possible. The herbs you buy from a grocery store or another gardener will still carry magical properties and will still perform well enough to get what you need done.

Many Wiccans would argue that working with your own garden and growing the herbs yourself is the best method for practicing Herbal Magic. For those of you ready to get your hands dirty and eager to learn, you don't need a wide back garden or a dedicated greenhouse. You can grow herbs on your balcony or windowsill if that is all that is what is available to you. Growing your own herbs is its own reward and this way you know that you are giving back to the Earth.

**Growing Directly from the Seed:**

Any good gardening book will have plenty of tips and tricks for growing your own herbs. Here are a few tips to get you started.

Most herb seeds will need to be germinated from 6-8 weeks before they are ready to be grown in the garden or a bigger pot. There are different methods used for germinating a seed, for one of them you will need:

- Cotton balls
- A glass jar or any small glass container as long as it is clean and clear
- Seeds

Step 1: Loosely fill the glass container with the cotton balls. Do not pack it too densely otherwise there will be no space for the seeds.

Step 2: Carefully drop the seeds into the glass container, making sure they are evenly distributed along the edge of the glass container and not hidden in the middle by the cotton balls. Try not to put too many seeds inside the container as each seed will need sufficient room to sprout out.

Step 3: Pour enough water into the glass container to wet the cotton balls and the seeds but not so much as there is an excess amount of water at the base of the container. If there is then pour it out.

Step 4: Place the glass container in a place where there is plenty of sunlight. Check the container each day to make sure that the cotton balls do not go dry. If they are dry, pour more water in just to make them damp but remember to pour any excess out.

The type of herb you are using depends on the amount of time it will need to germinate. Keep checking it as often as you can until you spot one of the seeds sprouting. The seed will split and a green stem or a leaf will start to grow out of the opening. Do not remove it yet as it is not ready. You need to wait until the roots of the plant appear, at which point the seeds will be too big for the glass container.

It is okay if not all the seeds you put in the glass container did not sprout the same time as the others did or even if they didn't sprout at all. You cannot leave the already sprouting seeds in the glass container while you wait for the others to sprout. You will risk killing the already growing plants and the other seeds might never germinate.

For the next few steps you will need the following:

- A few small or medium sized plant pots (you will need to plant single seeds in the small pots but if you wish to put several seeds in one pot then evenly space them out into a medium sized pot)
- The pots must be filled 3/4 of the way with sterilized potting soil (this is easy to buy in many stores)
- You will need a small amount of sterilized potting soil separate from the pots
- A small jar filled with clean water
- A clear and clean surface with which to work on

Step 5: Remove the cotton balls from the glass container one by one as carefully as possible. You'll find that a seed may have wrapped its roots around a cotton ball, do not tug at it but rather take the time to carefully unwind the roots.

Step 6: Take each seed and place it in the middle of its own small pot or place several of them evenly spaced apart and away from the edge of a medium pot. The roots of the seed must be placed directly on top of the potting soil.

Step 7: Carefully pour more soil into the pots, making sure to cover the roots of the herb and a little bit of the stem. The top of the herb must not be covered by any soil. If the herb has started growing any leaf, make sure those are above the soil.

Step 8: Pour water into the pot, wetting the soil but not over-watering it. Don't pour any water over the herb itself as it is sensitive at this point and taking in too much water could harm it. Place the pot in the sun and continue to water it as needed. How much sunlight and water it needs entirely depends on the herb you are growing.

For the second method you will need:

- 2-4 inch deep container (this can be anything from an egg carton, to a plastic tub)
- Sterilized potting soil
- Straws (optional)
- Some cling wrap

Step 1: Take your 2-4 inch container and poke a few small draining holes into the bottom. Make sure the holes aren't big enough for the soil to fall through but still allows for excess water to be drained.

Step 2: Fill the container with the sterilized potting soil and use the straws to make small indentation right in the middle of the container about half way down, (if you don't have a straw, you can do this with a small spoon or with the tip of your finger).

Step 3: Place a few seeds inside the indentation, using either the straw or drop them in carefully. Move some more soil over the seeds until they are fully covered.

Step 4: Put some cling wrap over the top of the container, making sure it is pulled tight and not touching the soil. This will stop the soil from drying out too quickly which will kill the seeds. Be sure to poke some holes in the cling wrap to allow for air flow, otherwise the seeds will not grow.

Step 5: Make sure you put the container somewhere it will get a lot of sunlight. At this point, the light is more important than the heat. So sunlight will help but not too much of it otherwise, once again, the soil will become too dry.

Step 6: Water as often as needed but make sure you don't drown the seeds with too much water. In the fragile germinating stage, too little or too much water could mean a lot to such a small seed.

For both methods, once the plants grow big enough, they may need to be moved to a bigger pot, depending on their size. Most herbs can live out their full cycles until they are harvested without the need to be transferred to a bigger pot.

Make sure to label the herbs if you are a beginner. It is difficult to tell one herb from another unless you are taught or teach yourself how to. You may remember which herbs you planted where but labeling them can ensure that there are no accidents. Labels will also help you keep track which plant needs what as each plant needs its own specific amount of care and attention.

Follow these steps and you will be well on your way to growing your own herbs and working side by side with nature. Do not worry if you do not succeed the first time, as mentioned, gardening is an art. You are creating life and working with a magic that is sensitive and fragile. Do not let failure stop you from trying again. In the end, you will be glad that you kept trying, when you see that first leaf sprout out of that seed and reach up towards the sun then it will all be worth it.

You will feel closer to the earth and all its magic, not to mention the gods themselves. So do yourself a favor as a Wiccan and do not deny yourself the opportunity to grow your own herbs and start up your own garden.

## HARVEST, DRY AND STORE YOUR HERBS

There is no closely guarded tradition or rule about what tool to use when harvesting your herbs. However, some traditions require a ritual tool of some kind but if yours doesn't then any kind of scissors or gardening snippers will do.

Keep in mind when wanting to harvest your herbs that the best time of day to do so is early in the morning. Preferably before the sun rises or before it is able to dry out the herbs. Doing this makes sure that the herb maintains its essential oils which comes in handy when using the herb for anything.

Basic Cutting: If you simply want to collect what you need for your work then only snip off the leaves or stems that you are going to use and no more. Some plants leaves, like basil, are easy to harvest as you can simply slide your fingers along the branch and pluck the leaves off. Other plants are sturdier and have wooden stems. With these plants, it is simpler to just snip the stem off completely to get to the leaves.

If you are harvesting things besides leaves and stems like flowers then it is best to wait until the flower has fully bloomed and has opened up. If you're after the seeds of a specific plant then you need to wait until the seeds are fully developed and dry on their own. Wrap a small bag over the head of the plant then shake until any dry seeds fall out into your bag. Fully developed seeds should fall out easily so don't force them by shaking the plant violently.

Remember that harvesting in the summer time is best as it promotes new growth of the plants you are harvesting.

Cutting in bunches: If you want to gather bundles of herbs then snip them off by the stems where they branch from the main plant. This will promote new growth in the plant and it will also make it easier to hang and dry out your herbs.

Drying Herbs: There are many methods to use when drying out your magical herbs.

Bunch your herbs up and tie them together by the stems. You can make your bundle as thick as you want by tying at least a dozen different stems together.

Hang the herbs out of the sunlight and in a dry, airy room. The direct sunlight could burn your herbs or over-dry them so it is best to hang them in a warm spot inside your home. They need to hang for about 3 weeks to dry, if they are not entirely dry then leave them for longer. The leaves will crack at your touch if the herbs are dry enough.

For the harvesting of seeds or blossoms from plants you are drying, use the same method as before. Put a bag below the head of the bundle you are drying and while the plant dries, the flowers and seeds of that plant should fall into the bag.

Another method you can use if you're in a hurry and prefer not to wait for three weeks is to simply pop the herbs into your oven. This however does pose a risk of burning your herbs altogether and the other method is much safer. Burnt herbs are rendered useless.

You must place your herbs, spread out evenly, on a cooking tray and put them in an oven. Make sure the oven is set on a low temperature to lower the risk of burning the herbs. This usually takes a few hours.

Storage of Herbs: Once the harvesting and drying method is complete, you will need to store any leftover herbs that weren't used. The wasting of magical herbs or any ingredients for that matter is something highly frowned upon amongst Wiccans.

The herbs need to be kept in an airtight container and out of the light. A colored glass or ceramic jar with an airtight lid will be perfect. Make sure to label the jars so you don't get confused on whether or not you put the Rosemary in the purple jar or the blue one. Labeling the jars will be safer especially if you're working with herbs that have toxic properties.

Once the herbs are in their respectively labeled jars, they will need to be placed in a cool, dry area. It is important that you keep the herbs away from any areas that you know will get hot for whatever reason.

## List of Common Magical Herbs and Their Properties

### Mugwort

Mugwort is an herb that is often used in modern Wiccan practices. It is an easy herb to grow and it is very versatile. It's useful for things like prophecies and it is used in divination rituals. It can be used in spellwork or as incense.

Magical properties of Mugwort are prophecy, divination, dreaming, and clairvoyance.

**Mugwort is harmful to pregnant women. Do Not handle, inhale, work with or eat Mugwort while you are pregnant.**

### Lavender

Lavender has been used by many people for centuries and not just in magickal rituals or Wiccan practices. It's a very easy plant to grow and also easy to harvest. It is usually associated with love spells or rituals. You can carry lavender with you or hang it around your house if you wish to bring love your way.

Magical properties of Lavender are love, peace, and calmness.

## Apples, or Apple Blossoms

There is a myth that an apple branch bearing the fruit, flowers, and an unopened bud was a key to the land of the Underworld.

The apple is a symbol of immortality amongst some ancients but it is also a symbol for death amongst others. Both the fruit and the blossoms can be used in Wiccan practices.

Magickal properties of Apples and Apple Blossoms are love and good luck.

## Basil

Basil is used for many things, in magickal spells and rituals and also culinary delights. It has been known far and wide for its easy use and tasty properties. It is not as well known for its magickal properties but it has many uses.

Magickal properties for Basil are purification, good luck and fortune, love divination, and fidelity.

## Rosemary

Rosemary is an herb that can be found in every kitchen, every garden, and in every Wiccan's collection. It was well known amongst ancient practitioners and was even used by Roman priests in ceremonies. It was also used in medicine to strengthen a patient's memory.

Magickal properties of Rosemary are protection from evil and negative energy, or can be used as incense for calming effects.

## Sage

The use of Sage can be dated back to ancient Greeks and Romans, who used to burn it because they believed that the smoke gave them wisdom. In magick terms, you can still burn the leaves and get similar effects but remember that the smell of burnt sage can be mistaken for the smell of marijuana.

Magickal properties of Sage include purification, clarity, guidance, promoting financial gain, and wishes.

## Chamomile

There are a few South American folk traditions that show chamomile as a lucky flower. It is associated with good luck in all things including love. It has many other uses and is fairly easy to grow and use.

Magickal properties of Chamomile are purification, protection, meditation, good luck and fortune, and love.

## Yarrow

Woundwort or Knight's Milfoil are names given to Yarrow by Scotland Highlanders. It was used to treat many battle wounds and injuries. When used in magickal workings, it has many other uses alongside its healing abilities. It has a bright yellow color which also makes for a beautiful garden in the spring time.

Its magickal properties include healing, love, psychic abilities, courage, passion in a marriage and it is also used to exorcize negative energies.

### Pennyroyal

Pennyroyal is very well known in the Wiccan practice as a magickal herb. In some Hoodoo magic, it was used for protection against something called the "evil eye." It is mostly used for protection magick although it also has uses in wealth and prosperity. It is not the easiest herb to grow but in this herb's case, a little goes a long way.

Magickal properties of Pennyroyal are protection, strength, and prosperity.

**Pennyroyal is harmful to pregnant women. Do not handle, inhale, work with, or eat Pennyroyal if you are pregnant.**

### Bay Leaf

Bay Leaves are extremely easy to grow and even easier to buy if you aren't very big on gardening. It can be used in simple magickal practices and rituals. The spells are easy to perform and are very effective when done correctly.

Magical properties include psychic visions, protection against evil and negative energy, dreams, and wishes.

### Cinnamon

This is very sweet and easy to come by ingredient is not only very useful in your kitchen but also in your spells and other magical creations. It's mostly used in wealth spells but it does have other uses.

Magical properties of Cinnamon are love, prosperity, luck, success, and it raises your spiritual vibrations.

## Patchouli

Most of this herb's fame has come from its scent. It is used in many rituals involving incense and potpourri. It is a popular herb that is used often by Wiccans. It has many magickal properties and its uses are varied.

Magickal properties of Patchouli are wealth and prosperity, sexual power and love, and it repels negative energy.

## Purple Dead Nettle

This herb is probably the easiest one you'll ever have growing in your garden. The way it grows and spreads, it's more like a weed than an herb and will take over your entire garden if not kept under control. It is easy to control if you are willing to keep an eye on it, but the work will be well worth the rewards. Purple Dead Nettle is not only a very useful and versatile plant but also, as the name suggests, its leaves are a deep shade of purple which makes for a fairly pretty garden view.

Keep in mind that although it is called nettle, it does not have the same qualities. It doesn't possess any stinging spikes and will not be able to harm you in any way. Also, be careful how much of this you have in your garden in the summer as it is a popular plant amongst the bees. It is also an annual plant so if you want to get rid of it then you can, it won't grow back, until more seeds find their way into your garden that is.

Magical Properties of Purple Dead Nettle are happiness and joy, it promotes will power and determination, ensures a healthy spirit and body. You can also use it for love, security, and prosperity.

**Warning! – Ingesting too much of Purple Dead Nettle can cause laxative effects, and pregnant or breastfeeding women are to keep away from it as it is unsafe for them and the baby.**

## Dandelion

This is more of a weed or a flower than it is an herb but it can be used the same way and provides many benefits. Whenever summer times come around and these bright yellow spots start to spread across everyone's lawns. it's usually a cause for panic. They invite a lot of bugs, including bees, and once you've got them it is difficult to get rid of them. So if you're stuck with them then why not take advantage of that.

Most see dandelions as a nuisance but a Wiccan will see it for what it is, a magickal ingredient for their next spell or ritual. It's easy to use and, as mentioned before, extremely easy to grow and or find.

Its magickal properties include health, wishes, and deviational dreams. It also promotes new beginnings and strength.

# CHAPTER 9
## DANGEROUS HERBS TO KEEP AWAY FROM

Wiccans use all sorts of herbs and plants in their rituals and spells, even the poisonous or otherwise dangerous ones. Even if these herbs can be harmful, their uses and magical properties are still valued by Wiccans. However, the practitioners that use these herbs are experienced and well read on how to handle these specific plants properly.

If you are new to the Craft and Herbal Magic then being cautious around these plants is a must. Unless you know what you are dealing with and are well experienced in the field then you should avoid the use of these plants entirely. If you do have a need for these plants and their specific qualities then seek professional help instead of trying to manage them yourself.

Some plants are harmful for specific reasons; plants like Basil may be perfectly fine for someone to use in their cooking but it can be harmful to a pregnant woman or a lactating woman. So here are lists of herbs that come with a "Warning" label.

The list will include the person directly affected by the plant and symptoms they can cause.

. . .

## Dangerous Herbs for Pregnant Women

If you're pregnant, trying to get pregnant or are nursing a baby, then this list is for you. You should be extremely careful around these herbs or avoid them altogether. These herbs can cause a range of symptoms and if they're ingested, they can even cause miscarriage. So heed this warning and take caution when eating, drinking or even handling these herbs with your bare hands.

*An underlined herb has an extremely dangerous effect.

- Basil; this herb can induce menstruation
- Catnip; this herb is known as a Uterine stimulant and can cause contractions
- Feverfew; this herb can also cause menstruation and may cause birth defects as well
- Angelica; this herb is also a Uterine stimulant and can cause contractions
- **Black cohosh**; This herb can cause a miscarriage, be extremely cautious
- Yarrow; this herb can cause menstruation
- **Mistletoe;** this herb can cause miscarriage, be extremely cautious
- **Goldenseal;** Can induce miscarriage
- Mugwort; this herb stimulates menstruation and can cause birth defects
- Pennyroyal; this herb is also a Uterine stimulant
- Rosemary; this herb is also a Uterine stimulant and can cause contractions
- **Comfrey;** this herb can cause liver damage for both the mother and the unborn baby

## Dangerous Herbs for Pets

Almost everyone owns a pet or lives around people who do have pets. All Wiccans love animals as they are part of the many natural cycles, and one of the philosophies that every Wiccan lives by is the policy against negative energy and harming others.

So here is a list of herbs that aren't dangerous to the humans using or working with them but can be harmful to the animal life around you. So act carefully and be cautious about the animal life around you while you work.

- Buckeye; this herb can cause diarrhea and vomiting in cats and dogs, if consumed on a regular basis it can cause seizures and muscular tremors
- Holly berries; this herb can lead to drooling, head shaking, and gastrointestinal upset in both dogs and cats
- **Foxglove;** this herb can lead to an elevated or even abnormal heart rate, arrhythmias, and, in extreme circumstances, death in dogs and cats
- Jimson weed; this herb is dangerous and harmful to not just cats and dogs but also horses and other larger animals. It can lead to light sensitivity, anxiety, restlessness, and dilated pupils
- Chamomile; this herb can lead to diarrhea and vomiting in cats and dogs
- **Tobacco**; this herb can lead to moderate or severe vomiting; it can cause an abnormal or elevated heart rate, or respiration. It can cause overstimulation, or paralysis and it can even lead to death in dogs and cats
- **Pennyroyal;** with this herb the dried up leaves are harmless, however, the oil it produces can cause liver failure if it is eaten. It can also cause a miscarriage in pregnant cats
- **Mistletoe berries**; this herb is associated with

vomiting, abdominal pain, and diarrhea in dogs and cats. When ingested in excessive amounts, it can cause death.

## Keep Yourself Safe

Most would advise the total avoidance of all these herbs, unless you have the proper qualifications and experience to handle and work with them. Although, even with all the warnings and words of caution there are some who would still try their hand anyways and use these herbs. Instead of hoping that this won't happen, here are some tips on keeping yourself and those around you safe.

There are various ways to avoid putting yourself, people around you, or any animal life in danger with herbs, and all of them use a certain amount of common sense.

The first thing you have to do is make sure you are familiar with all the herbs and the side effects they cause, before you start using them. I would recommend investing in a book or full guide to herbs and plants, so you can make sure you are fully prepared for what can happen.

The second and most important thing to keep in mind is if you are working with a herb that is completely unfamiliar to you then avoid ingesting it in anyway. Even if it looks or smells harmless, if you are unfamiliar with it and the side effects it can cause then it's better to not risk it.

There are many other ways you can use a herb that will utilize its full magical properties and you can avoid ingesting them completely. You can make sachets to keep your herbs in, dress candles with them, and much more. Unless you are certain that it is safe to drink or eat the herb then avoid it entirely.

The main thing to remember is to practice extreme caution and use common sense when dealing with herbs. Even if you are familiar with herbs, I still recommend a small amount of safety. If you have even the slightest of doubt in any of the herbs and your safety while using it then don't use it at all.

**Magickal Creations: Teas, Brews, Oils, Baths, and More…**

There are several forms of magick other than spells. Some magic requires recipes instead of incantations. There are magickal creations you can eat and drink, such as herbal teas, in order to reach your magickal goal. You can make your own candles and other tools to place at your Altar that should heighten your spells and ensure success in your other forms of magick.

There are plenty of magickal creations to keep you busy if you are a lover of crafts and DIY projects. If you aren't a very handy person, there are some magickal creations that are simple enough even for someone with no previous skill in such a field.

There baths, oils, incenses, dream sachets and many more things that you can do that requires little to no previous knowledge on crafting. As with every form of magick, especially magickal creations, there is still the Wiccan Rede and Rule of Three to keep in mind when doing anything.

**Teas and Brews and other Concoctions**

The Perfect Brew

If you are just starting out with herbal magick then tea is probably the best place for beginners. This is just a few tips and tricks to help you with your brewing journey. Tea, especially magickal herbal tea, is a form of art and requires a precise method. Most beginners and newcomers like to start with herbal teas and brews so here are some tips to help you along the way.

**Warm your teapot or the cup** you'll be drinking from before you start – this will help maintain the temperature of the tea while it's brewing. It takes very little effort but it makes a really big difference in the long run.

There isn't a special type of cup or teapot you should use, what you prefer is what matters. If you like using an old mug then go ahead, if you prefer to use the dainty china then that works as well.

**Overboiling is bad** so try not to do it – overboiling drains the water of oxygen. For normal tea, overboiling isn't a problem but when working with herbs and trying to infuse the tea with their magickal properties then there is a certain temperature you should work with.

Just below the boiling point which is as low as 70 degrees Celsius is a perfect temperature for most plants. If you are using a kettle however, you should turn it off once the water starts rumbling; this should put it at an ideal temperature.

**The perfect time for the perfect brew** – you'll need to adjust your brewing time depending on the type of herb or plant you are using. This is where the trial and error comes into play. You don't want to over-brew or under-brew a tea as it can affect the taste and magickal properties of the herb; you'll need to put some practice into this step. Although, if you are ever at a loss, then the standard brew time for most herbs is 10-15 minutes.

·  ·  ·

**To sweeten or not to sweeten** – if you prefer your tea to be sweetened then by all means you can add some sugar or honey or other forms of sweetener. However, sugar is the best choice as it simply sweetens the tea where other sweeteners like honey add an extra taste to the tea. This could affect the overall taste of the herbal tea and you may not want to drink it.

When making your own tea at home using herbs and other plants, there are two ways to do this. You can either use infusions or decoctions, both of which require time and practice in order to get it right. Don't worry though; it is a well-rewarded task if you are willing to put in the work.

Tea for Love

This is a simple tea you can make and drink to bring love your way. The ingredients are simple and should be in your Wiccan garden, if not you can always go get some from any store.

Ingredients:

- Rose petals
- Caraway seeds
- Fennel
- Tea (any kind you like)
- Tea infuser

Instructions:

Step 1: Boil some pure water and make yourself a cup of tea. You can make any kind of tea you like, green tea, black tea, you're going to be drinking it so what you like matters. Don't fill the cup up as you'll need to add a little more water.

Step 2: You'll need a tea infuser because you want to get the flavour of the other ingredients into the tea but you don't want to take a sip and get a rose petal in your mouth.

Rinse the rose petals with some pure water to make sure they are clean. Mix the caraway seeds, fennel and a few rose petals together and place them in the tea infuser. Lower the tea infuser into the tea you have already brewed and add a little more boiled water.

Leave the tea infuser for as long as you feel is necessary for the full flavor of the ingredients to blend with the tea. Time is very important when it comes to infusing tea, it is an art that requires trial and error and a bit of practice.

Step 3: Once you've removed the tea infuser, you should be able to smell all those flavors mixed together. You can add some milk and sugar if you want but you don't have to if you prefer your tea black and unsweetened.

Step 4: Sit down somewhere comfortable with your cup of hot, fresh tea in your hand. Repeat this incantation:

I lift this cup to my lips, I drink it slow with tiny sips, rose, tea, caraway, and fennel cause love to stay.

This is a very simple and effective tea you can make any time if you need to bring a little bit of love into your life.


Moon Tonic

Tonic water that has been infused with the powerful energies of the moon is great for healing and bringing balance to the body, the mind, and the soul. It's simple and requires a few ingredients.

Ingredients:

- Some cool water (rain or spring, as long as it's fresh)
- A clear quartz crystal
- Some clear plastic wrap
- A glass
- A clear sky and a full moon

Instructions:

Step 1: On a clear night with a full moon, put your crystal in a clear glass and measure out one cup of your purified water to put in the glass. Make sure you've checked for the exact time the sun will be setting on the day you've chosen to perform this ritual.

Step 2: Cover the glass with the plastic wrap so no bugs or dust can fly into the water. At sundown, precisely place the glass in a safe place outdoors in a moonlit area. Make sure nothing will block it from the moon light during the night.

Step 3: Remove the glass of water at dawn; if it was left all night in the clear moonlight then it should now be infused with the magickal properties of the lunar cycle.

You can drink the moon water every morning to prepare your mind, body, and soul for the stress and strife of the day ahead.


Wassail without Alcohol

This is a hot beverage usually drank during the Wiccan Yule celebrations. This tradition comes from ancient times where families would go out wassailing on a cold winter's eve. Back then, it was meant to be a blessing of good health and fortune to your neighbours and friends and they would usually be offered a mug of warm cider or ale at the door. However, this has since evolved into what we call Christmas carolling today.

There are many recipes, some involving eggs and alcohol while others go without both but the basic beverage and its properties of good health, fertility, protection, and good luck, still remain the same.

Ingredients:

- Nutmeg
- Allspice
- Three cinnamon sticks or three table spoons of ground cinnamon
- Ginger
- Whole cloves
- Two oranges
- One apple (peeled and diced)
- Two cups of cranberry juice
- One gallon of apple cider
- Half a cup of sugar
- Half a cup of honey

Instructions:

Step 1: Set your crockpot (which is a traditional method) or stove to its lowest setting. Pour in the apple cider, cranberry juice, sugar, and honey and mix together slowly. As it heats up, you'll need to stir continuously so the sugar and honey can dissolve properly.

Step2: Take the oranges and stud them with the cloves and then place them in the pot carefully. They should float. Then add the diced apple.

Step 3: Add the ginger, nutmeg, and allspice until you like the taste, usually a few teaspoons of each is enough but you can add more depending on how you like it. Then snap the cinnamon sticks in half and throw them in or just sprinkle in the three tablespoons of ground cinnamon.

Step 4: Cover the pot, keeping the heat on the lowest setting, and leave the ingredients to shimmer for about 2-4 hours. You can now serve it when you are ready to but make sure you serve it while it is still hot.

For the alcoholic version of this recipe, simply add half a cup or one cup of brandy to the pot at least half an hour before serving. Make sure it is properly mixed in so that one cup doesn't have a stronger taste of brandy in it than another does.

### Sip of Tea for Success

While you drink this tea, you must envision yourself being successful at any current task you are dealing with. If you can picture yourself succeeding while you sip at this tea then the success you seek will find its way to you.

Ingredients:

- One ginger root
- Two lemon balm leaves
- Four clover flowers

Instructions:

Step 1: Boil some water and warm up your cup or teapot, whatever you'll be drinking out of. When the water is boiled, pour it into your prepared cup.

Step 2: Place the ingredients into a tea infuser and slowly lower it into the boiling water. Leave it to brew for an appropriate amount of time, remember not too long and not too short a time.

Step 3: Remove the tea infuser once the ingredients have been properly infused into the boiling water. Add milk or sweetener as desired and it's ready to drink.

## Protection Brew **(Do not drink!)**

This is a brew for protection of the home against evil spirits and negative energy. It is extremely simple to make but it is not for consumption and should be thrown away as soon as you are finished with it.

Ingredients:

- One part Hyssop
- One part Vetiver
- One part Mistletoe
- Two parts Rosemary
- Three parts Rue

Instructions:

Step 1: Brew all the ingredients together in a big pot, no need to use a tea infuser for this. Simply place all the ingredients in the pot with some boiling water and stir until you're sure that the herbs have fused with the water thoroughly.

Step 2: Strain the water to get rid of all the bits and pieces of the ingredients. All you need is the herb infused water.

Step 3: Use the water to anoint all the windowsills and doorframes of your house. You can anoint any other part of your house that you feel needs protection from negativity and evil. Pour what you haven't used down the drain. Whatever you do, you can't drink the water as some of the herbs in this recipe are toxic.

## Seven Flower Tea

This is a cooling and calming tea that you can make out of fresh herbs from your garden or dried herbs from your Wiccan cupboard. You can also buy the herbs if you don't have them on hand.

Ingredients:

- One teaspoon lavender flower
- One teaspoon linden flower
- One teaspoon honeysuckle flower
- One teaspoon calendula flower
- One and a half teaspoon orange flower (or orange peel)
- One and a half teaspoon passion flower
- Two teaspoons chamomile flower
- One quart of boiling water

Instructions:

Step 1: Place all the flowers into a container (metal preferably so it will keep its warmth), then pour the boiling water over the flowers.

Step 2: Leave the flowers in the water for about 20 minutes to allow all the magical properties to seep out into the water.

Step 3: Strain the water and throw away the flowers. You can drink the water as is, if it isn't sweet enough for you then add some sugar or another kind of sweetener. I do not recommend adding milk to this brew.

Rainbow Brew

For this, you'll need to wait for it to rain. Watch the skies and wait for there to be a break in the clouds and you can see a rainbow. If you see a rainbow and it is still raining then place a non-metallic pan or container outside so it can catch some rain.

If you catch some rain during the presence of a rainbow then the rain water is now blessed by the rainbow and you can save that water for rituals. Because the rainbow is made up of all colors, the rain water can be used for all kinds of magick.

Make sure to bottle it up, label it, and keep it somewhere safe and cool until an opportunity arises to use it. This Rainbow Brew can be added to your bath water during rituals or you can use it to anoint your body or hands while keeping your magickal goal in mind.

Sleep Brew

If you're having trouble sleeping and are plagued by constant nightmares then this simple tea is perfect for you. It helps settle your body and if you use it before bed each night, you should be free of nightmares.

Ingredients:

- One part Vervain
- One part Rose petals
- One part Myrtle leaves

Instructions:

Step 1: Fill a pot with water and soak a few rose petals in it for three days adding more petals every day.

Step 2: On the third day at sunrise, add the other two ingredients (the vervain and myrtle) and leave it to soak all day.

Step 3: That night before you go to bed, soak a clean cloth in three handfuls of the brew and bathe your forehead with it.

You should have no trouble falling asleep and you won't be bothered by nightmares.

Use the brew each night before you go to bed until it is all gone, then you can make another batch.

**Bath Salts, Rituals, and other Stuff**

Prosperity Bath

Some spells require you to take a bath as it allows the body to relax and the magickal energy within you will be able to flow freely. This is one of the simple bath spells as it doesn't require you to make anything specific and you'll only need a few supplies.

Ingredients:

- Salt
- One green candle (this represents wealth)
- A few coins
- A sharp tool or ritual knife

Instructions:

Run yourself a nice warm bath, no need for any bubble bath but if you want to add it then go ahead. While the bath is running, use a sharp tool or ritual knife to carve the amount of money you are seeking into the side of the candle. If you are not expecting a specific amount of money then you can just carve the word "Wealth" into the side of the candle. Place the candle, salt, and coins at your Altar and charged them with energy while you are waiting for the bath.

When you are ready, just add a pinch of salt and the coins to your bathwater then light the candle and place it at the edge of the bath. Be careful where you put it so it doesn't fall in.

Turn off all the lights, hop on in, get relaxed and try to visualize the money coming to you. When you feel you are focused on your goal and you're ready then say this incantation:

The green dragon flies over the sea, bring wealth and prosperity to me.

Allow the candle to burn ¼ of the way then you can hop out of the bath. Place the candle and coins at your Altar and allow the candle to burn all the way down. If the spell was a success then you should receive some money in your future.

## Wealth Attraction Bath

You can use this bath mixture any time but its magickal properties are more effective if you use it before an event where you're expecting some money. A bank visit for example.

Ingredients:

- A small vial or a bottle with a tightly sealed lid
- Three drops of basil oil
- Three drops of pine oil
- Three drops of cinnamon oil
- A sprinkling of patchouli herb
- A handful of sea salt

Instructions:

Run a warm bath for yourself, you can add any bubble bath or some candles if you want to (green candles are best), whatever helps you relax. Add the salt, herbs, and oils to the warm water and get in. Soak in the water for about 15 minutes; while you're in the bath try to think about the situation you'll be entering today. Think about what you want the outcome to be and try to visualize your financial success.

Get out of the bath but don't let the water drain out just yet. Take the small vial or bottle and fill it with some of the water first. Seal the lid tightly so nothing leaks out and take the vial with you on your visit to the bank as a symbol of wealth and good luck in your success.

Herbal Protection Bath

This is a spell to add a little bit of protection to yourself, not your home like other spells or to someone else. You should be able to find all the herbs you need in your Wiccan garden.

Ingredients:

- Lavender
- Rosemary
- Basil
- Rue
- Mint
- Some coarse salt
- A small bowl

Instructions:

Fill the bath with hot water, not too hot but a comfortable warm or whatever temperature you prefer your baths to be. Toss all the herbs and the coarse salt into the water and let the bath steep for a couple of minutes. Once you've gotten in, you can sit back and soak in the water, visualize your body being filled with the protective energy being drained from the herbs into the water.

You can stay in the bath for as long as you feel is necessary to absorb all that protective energy. Before you drain the water, take the bowl and save a little bit of the water with some of the herbs and toss it outside for that extra bit of protection.

. . .

Personal Purification Bath

This is an herbal bath to purify your body and spirit of all negative energy you may have been exposed to during the day. This helps when you've spent time with unpleasant people or a negative influence in your life.

Ingredients:

- Fennel
- Rosemary
- Anise seed
- Hyssop
- White sage
- Cedar oil
- A square of cheesecloth
- A small bowl

Instructions:

The exact measurements of the herbs aren't important and it's up to you at the end of the day, but usually about a tablespoon of each should be enough.

Mix all of the herbs together in a small bowl and then put a few drops of the cedar oil into the bowl. Stir it some more until everything is properly blended and then bundle it up in cheesecloth. You can make this in bulk and keep the cheesecloth in a safe, cool place until the need arises to take a purification bath.

Run a hot bath and place the cheesecloth filled with the herbs into the water; do not add any other bath products. You must allow yourself sufficient time to soak in the herbal bath, about an hour should be enough time. This should clear away all the negative energy that your body and spirit have absorbed. Dispose of the cheesecloth and herbs after your bath.

<u>Wash Away a Curse</u>

This spell is a bit more difficult than other spells or rituals but it will get the job done. If you feel like bad luck always seems to find its way to you and it's starting to seem as if you're cursed, then this is the perfect bath for you.

Ingredients:

- Twelve white candles
- One dark purple or black candle
- One tablespoon of lavender blossoms
- One tablespoon of chamomile
- One tablespoon of white sage not green sage
- One cup of coarse salt

Instructions:

This spell must be performed on the night after the full moon if you want the best results. Go to your Altar and make a circle with the twelve white candles and put the black or dark purple on in the middle. Don't light the candles yet.

Run a hot bath, add the herbs and the salt, and then light the candles. You can make the circle of candles by your Altar or directly in the bathroom to save time. After you light the candles get into the bath, sit back and get comfortable. Say the following incantation:

*By the light of moon's wane*

*Cleanse my soul of this strain*

*Let the spell be reversed*

*Lift away this dark curse*

*As I enter a sacred space*

*Return my soul to grace*

Pour some of the bath water over your head keeping your eyes closed tight or just hold your breath and dunk your head under the water. Be very careful not to get any of the water in your eyes. Do this precisely three times then say:

*I forgive what was done*

*Let the spell be undone*

Remain in the bath until the water starts to feel cool. Get out of the bath and blow out all of the candles but do not disturb their circle. For the following three nights, light all the candles again and repeat the last part of the chant:

*I forgive what was done*

*Let the spell be undone*

After the third night, light the black candle, which represents the curse and let it burn down naturally if it hasn't already.


## Happiness Ritual Bath

You'll need a colored candle for this spell; bathing by candle light is more effective as the light is provided by the flame is more natural than your fluorescent lighting. You can have the ritual bath in the day then you can use the natural light of the sun and have no need for a candle.

For the happiness ritual bath, the color of the candle you use is important as certain colors are associated with happiness and joy. Choosing the right color will help to ensure the effectiveness of the bath.

Yellow is associated with joy, happiness, self-esteem, hope, and sunshine.

Orange is associated with success, joy, and it promotes stimulation.

Blue is associated with calmness, peace, and tranquillity.

For this bath, you can choose whichever colored candle you feel fits your needs and goals best.

Ingredients for the Herbal Mixture:

- A quarter cup of rose petals
- A quarter cup of jasmine flowers
- One cup of Epsom salt
- You can add a few drops of either rose, jasmine, or lavender oil but it is not necessary
- Things you need:
- Wine (optional)
- Candles for light and your choice of colored candle
- Music (something that will calm you, try natural sounds like rain)
- A bath

Instructions:

Run some hot water for a bath and put the ingredients in the water, if you wish to add oils in, do so separately from the other ingredients. Put your choice of music on (keep the electronics far away from the water) and light all the candles except for your colored candle.

Get in the bath, sit back and relax. Practice breathing deeply and thinking only calm and soothing thoughts. If you can, try to keep your mind blank as you focus on the music in the background. When you feel you are ready, hold your colored candle in your hand and light it. Repeat this incantation as you hold the candle:

*Water run and river flow*

*Goddess I call you here*

*Bad thoughts I let you go*

*I am calm and have no fear*

Place the candle down and close your eyes. Allow yourself to relax completely, trust that you are safe in your space. When you are ready, you can get out of the bath and drain the water. If it is safe and you wish to leave the candles to burn down naturally then you can.

## Oils

Essential oils made from various herbs, flowers, and other plants, and can be very useful when it comes to all forms of magick. You use oils in spells, baths, rituals, anointing, and so much more. A vial of essential oil can be a Wiccan's most useful tool or ingredient if they know not only how to use it but how to make it.

Most recipes call for the herbal or floral ingredients to be added to 1/8 cup of base oil. Most commonly used oils are Almond Oil, Apricot Oil, Grapeseed Oil, and others. The recipes for oils are usually extremely simple but they don't make a lot so you'll have to work to keep your stocks full.

### Come and See Me Oil

This oil is used in a simple ritual to attract the attention of an ideal partner.

Ingredients:

- Five drops of Patchouli
- One drop of Cinnamon
- 1/8 cup of Olive oil

Instructions:

Mix the ingredients together in a saucepan and let it simmer on low heat until all the ingredients are combined. You can tell by the strong smell and the thickening of the oil. Strain the oil to make sure all the herb remains are out and it is smooth.

Smear on a white candle and burn the candle while visualizing the ideal partner you wish to attract.

## Oil for Courage

This is a simple oil recipe you can put into a vial and wear on you to bring you that extra bit of courage for nerve wracking situations.

Ingredients:

- Three drops of Ginger
- One drop of Black pepper
- One drop of Clove
- Any base oil

## Oil to Invoke the Powers of Earth

You can place this oil in a vial and wear it on you to invoke the magical properties of the element Earth. This will bring to you money, prosperity, stability, abundance, and foundation.

Ingredients:

- Four drops of Patchouli
- Four drops of Cypress
- Any base oil

## Oil for Good luck

Ingredients:

- Half a teaspoon of powdered Mandrake wood
- Three teaspoons of ground nutmeg
- One tablespoon of dried Wormwood
- A quarter cup of Olive Oil base
- Thirteen drops of Pine

Allow the oil to sit for thirteen nights after making it. Put it in a vial and wear it on you to ensure good luck.

## Oil for Interviews

Wear this oil in a vial when you are going to an interview of any kind. It helps to calm you and make a favorable impression.

Ingredients:

- One drop Rose
- Three drops Lavender
- Four drops of Ylang-Ylang
- Any base oil

## Draw Love Oil

Wear in a vial on you to draw love your way or anoint a pink candle and burn it while visualizing the love you want.

Ingredients:

- One drop of Ginger
- One drop of Cardamom
- Two drops of Rosemary
- Five drops of Ylang-Ylang
- Seven drops of Palma

### Moon Oil

You can use this oil to speed healing, induce psychic dreams, increase fertility, facilitate sleep, and many other influences of the moon. You can wear it during a full moon to connect with its lunar energy and heighten your own power.

Ingredients:

- One drop Rose
- One drop Jasmine
- Any base oil

### Peace Oil

If you feel nervous or upset, you can put this oil in a vial and wear it on you to calm you down. You can also stand in front of a mirror, and anoint yourself with the oil while looking into your own eyes.

Ingredients:

- One drop of Rose Absolute

- Two drops of Chamomile
- Three drops of Ylang-Ylang
- Three drops of Lavender
- Any base oil

Power Oil

This oil is great if you wish to add that extra bit of power to yourself during crucial or difficult rituals. Anoint yourself with the power oil before performing these rituals.

Ingredients:

- One drop Ginger
- One drop Pine
- Four drops Orange
- Any base oil

**Charms**

Charms are very useful in Wiccan magick and you'll find that they come in all different forms and sizes. Most Wiccans make their own Charm bags or sachets and these can have whatever use the Wiccan desires.

A Charm can be worn on the body for any reason, whether it is love, luck, protection, or something else entirely. A Charm can be placed underneath one's pillow to induce psychic influences and/or dreams of divination. There are also charms that are hung around the house or on front doors for various forms of protection or other reasons.

For whatever reason a Charm is used for, they are usually simple to make and their magickal properties not only vary but they normally last for an exceptional amount of time. Most charms require the use of flower petals, herbs, or other plants so you will be spending a lot of time in your Wiccan garden and kitchen.

Flower Petal Love Charm

This is a charm to hang somewhere you spend a lot of time so its magickal energy can rub off on you. You can hang it somewhere in your bedroom or even your bathroom, just make sure it's safe from unexpected events wherever it is.

Ingredients:

- Rose petals
- Lavender petals
- Daffodil petals
- Poppy petals
- Honeysuckle petals
- Chamomile petals
- Carnation petals
- Geranium petals
- Five apple seeds
- A small, transparent pink bag

You don't need petals from all the flowers for the charm to do its job but you do need petals from at least five of the flowers. Make sure the back is transparent and made up of some kind of mesh; it needs plenty of air holes so that the air can flow through it freely.

Instructions:

Step 1: Measure out about a tablespoon of each petal, making sure to keep the different petals separate. Drop each petal into the bag one by one, it may be tedious but it's the right way to do it.

Step 2: As you drop each flower petal into the bag, repeat the lines "He loves me" for one petal and then "He loves me not" for another petal, (an oldie but a Goldie). Make sure you end with "He loves me" or the charm might bring unwanted results.

Step 3: Put in the five apple seeds, no need to drop these ones in one at a time you can just drop them in. Close the bag up tightly and hang it up either in your bedroom or bathroom.

If you want to further its success in bringing you love, you can place it where the wind can blow through it more frequently, releasing that energy on a regular basis. Make sure it's safe and won't be knocked over or blown about. Leave the charm there for about a month and no longer.

As the Tree Grows Fortune Charm

This is a charm that uses the strength of a growing tree to grow your personal fortune with it. Remember as with all fortune, prosperity, or money magick, if you are greedy then the magick is more likely to backfire, this will bring harm rather than help. Only perform prosperity and fortune magick if you are in need of it.

Ingredients:

- A small green bag (cotton preferably but any natural fabric will do)
- A coin
- A smooth rock
- An acorn
- Four small white feathers (real, not synthetic)
- Paper and Pencil

Instructions:

Step 1: Take the paper and pencil and write your name out, write it in a way so that the letters form a circle. Draw a small pentacle in the centre of the circle then fold it up and place it in the charm bag.

Step 2: Draw a pentacle on the small stone and acorn as well then put them in the charm bag also. Next put in the coin and the feathers, no need to draw a pentacle on those ingredients.

Step 3: Tie up the bag tightly and hold it up in between your palms. Repeat the following incantation out loud and clear:

*As the tall tree grows, so does my fortune*

*As the sun rises high, so does my fortune*

*By this charm, I do begin*

*Magick starts to grow within*

Step 4: Take the charm outside; if you have a yard with trees in it then you can simply place the charm by a tree where you know it won't be disturbed. If you don't have any private trees in your yard then you can go find a tree somewhere else. The charm bag must be safe from people removing it or throwing it away so stay clear of any trees in a public park. Perhaps try the woods or maybe even a friend's house if they have trees, and with their permission of course.

Loosely tie the charm bag to a branch of your chosen tree as high as you can get it without putting yourself in harm's way. After you've hung it up, repeat the above incantation again and the deed is done.

If the charm bag was made correctly, new financial success should start to come to you, keep in mind it may take some time. Trees grow at their own pace.

Money Dream Charm

This charm isn't designed to bring you fortune or financial success but if done the right way, it can bring you dreams that will guide you on your way to financial security. Although it won't bring you any new wealth, it can show you the right path to take on your way there.

Ingredients:

- A small green cloth bag
- Mint
- Mugwort
- Cedar
- Dill
- Patchouli
- Lavender
- Pine oil

Instructions:

Step 1: Place all the ingredients into the green cloth bag, one by one. You don't need a lot of each herb and make sure that the bag is not bulging or overfilled. The herbs must be able to move around loosely once you've tied the bag shut.

Step 2: Take your pillow or you can use another pillow if you don't want to get any oil on the pillow you use regularly. Put a few drops of the Pine oil on the pillow, inside the pillow if that is possible and not on the pillow case itself.

Step 4: Place the green cloth bag filled with herbs underneath your pillow before you go to bed and light a green candle. Make sure it's somewhere safe and let it burn down naturally while you are asleep.

You can expect to receive dreams that will point you down the path to financial success.

· · ·

## Friendship Charm

If you need a little bit of help strengthening that bond between you and your friends then this charm bag is sure to help.

Ingredients:

- A small yellow cloth bag
- Pineapple leaves
- Dried orange rind
- Dried lemon rind

Instructions:

Simply combine all the ingredients into the yellow cloth bag and seal it tightly. You can carry the charm around in your purse or tuck it away underneath your pillow. Or just keep it somewhere that's nearby where it will be safe and its magickal energy can flow freely.

## Herb Bundle of Protection

This is also considered a charm of sorts; it's a bundle of herbs that you can make to hang on your door or by your windows. This charm can protect your house from negative energy or spirits or outside entities that wish you harm. Most herb bundles are made up of just one herb but for extra protection, you can bundle a few herbs together that have the same protective properties.

Ingredients:

- Sage (it has a purifying and cleansing effect)
- Chamomile (this herb is known for its purification and protection)
- Hyssop (used as a defence against negative energy)

- Patchouli (well known for its repelling power and defense against negative energy)
- Rosemary (this herb has been used for protection against evil spirits since Roman times)
- A strip of cloth long enough to tie around the bundle

Instructions:

You don't have to use all of the herbs listed above, but for the most success in protecting your home, I recommend you try to use most of them. This bundle can be messy to make so you might want to find an appropriate workspace or use your Altar.

Step 1: Take all the herbs you are going to use in this bundle. It's best if they have been harvested and dried by you but you can buy some if you don't have any on hand. The bundle must be made up of at least one part of each herb but you can put more of a certain herb in if you want its quality to shine out more.

Step 2: Place one dried herb down on top of the strip of cloth and wrap the cloth around the tip of it. Place another herb next to that one and repeat the process, wrapping the cloth around the tip of both the herbs. Keep doing this until all the herbs have been bunched together with the strip of cloth tied securely around their tips and spiralling upward.

Step 3: Now that your bundle is secured tightly and all the herbs are tied together, you can light a candle (the color isn't important, white is good enough for this) and burn stick the tip of the bundle in the flame. Be careful that the flame doesn't touch the cloth and that you don't burn the herbs. You just want it to smoke a little at the end then you can blow the flame out.

Step 4: While the herbs are still smoking, you can hang the bundle up on your front door. You can hang it outside the door but it is better that you keep it on the inside of your house. With your Bundle Charm of Protection hanging up, your home is now protected against negative energy, evil spirits and other things that wish to do you harm.

You can use a flame to light up the edge of the bundle again if you want to release that extra bit of its energy. Just be careful not to burn the herbs or the cloth tied around them.

Bundle Charm for Love

This is the same as the bundle of herbs for protection but instead we use herbs that have properties associated with love. The methods and steps are exactly the same as the bundle above the only thing that's different is the herbs you use.

Ingredients:

- Apple branches, preferably with blossoms (the apple plant is known for many things but love is the most prominent of its qualities)
- Lavender stalks (this herb is often associated with love spells and magick among other things)
- Purple Dead Nettle (known for many things, love being one of them and it's pretty)
- Patchouli (love is one of the things this herb is least known for but it can still be useful in this bundle)
- A long strip of cloth (pink preferably but it's not necessary)

Once again you don't have to use all of the herbs in this list to make your bundle charm and you can even substitute the herbs for others you know to have magickal properties of love. At the end of the day, magick bundle is for you and you can add and remove any herbs you want.

After you've made the bundle, you can hang it anywhere in your home to promote feelings of love and perhaps bring a new love interest in your life.

There are many other magickal creations, such as making your own candles for rituals and spells. There are things known as Poppets in Wiccan culture, they are similar to the Voodoo dolls you see in popular movies however I always found their purpose to be a bit dark for the Wiccan way. Poppets are also very difficult to work with and require a lot of practice before you can use them in a spell or ritual correctly.

These recipes are simple starters to get you on your way to where you want to be. Soon you'll be writing down your own spells and recipes in your own Book of Shadows. Once you get the hang of it, you'll find there is a simple science to all this magick and it's easy to grasp if you try your best.

No matter what you do on your path to the divine, make sure you keep in mind the Wiccan Rede and the Rule of Three. For your safety and the safety of those around you.

# CHAPTER 10
# A GUIDE TO SUCCESSFUL SPELLCASTING

A core element of the Wiccan religion lies in magical creations and spellcasting. There are some who take part in the practices but do not participate in spellwork or magickal creations, this is normal. The magical elements of being a Wiccan is not a necessary element; you can participate in the rituals and worship the deities without needing to take part in anything related to magick.

One of the most common problems when it comes to newcomers to the religion is a spell not working. This is understandable as the art of spellcasting is not straightforward and if you do not have experience then something like this is bound to happen. However, I will say that no matter what you think happened or didn't happen when you were casting a spell or working with magick, it always works.

When it comes to any form of magick, people assume that it's a straight path from A to B, however, this isn't exactly true. When you cast a spell with a goal in mind, the magick will take every path available to it in order to get to its destination. Its ultimate goal is to find the path of less resistance to get to the goal you had in mind when you cast the spell, but there is a catch to this process.

Since there are so many paths for the magick to travel down then that means that there are many destinations for it to reach. In this case, it is easier for the Wiccan casting the spell to try and be as specific as they can; however, this is not always as simple as it sounds.

In the end, your spell did work, just not in the way you were hoping it would. When casting a spell, there are a number of outcomes. And even though you are hoping for a particular outcome, it won't always be at the end of the path the magick decides to take for you.

**What is a Spell?**

The first thing you need to understand is what a spell is exactly. You've probably watched a movie where someone has incanted some kind of poem that rhymed nicely and there was probably a creepy howling sound accompanied by a stray, cold breeze through the window. Or perhaps someone waved their hand or wand shouting a command in a language you've never heard before and they made a book fly across the room or unlocked a door. This is not the magick you'll be working with in the Wiccan religion; this is the stuff of fiction but that doesn't mean that a spell cast by a Wiccan is any less magickal.

A spell is not a poem, or incantation, or a command you can shout into the universe and expect to get exactly what you wanted almost as soon as you asked for it. Movies like Practical Magic are more similar to the practices of Wiccans.

When you cast a spell, you are preparing yourself to go after what it is you want to spell to grant you and then you are using the spell to direct the magical energy so it can clear a path for you to reach what you want. You can't cast a spell and expect the results you want to fall out of the sky and land in your lap, the magick of the universe just doesn't work that way.

**Basic Tips for Spell Casting**

1. You receive what you give – whatever you are thinking about is what will be attracted to you. Like attracts like, so if you are thinking negative thoughts while casting a spell then you will inadvertently attract negativity your way. This happens even if you don't mean it to; perhaps you are casting a spell with the intent to wish away something negative, like a problem or a bad habit, by focusing on it you will instead do the opposite. If you are attempting to rid yourself of something negative then instead of focusing on the thing you want to be rid of try putting your focus on something you want instead, something positive that you would hope to replace the negativity. Or think of how positive and good life will be once you have rid yourself of that negative energy.

2. Be faithful and have no doubts – You spell can only be successful if you give it complete and unwavering certainty that it will be successful. You cannot cast a spell and hope for the best, or start thinking about plan B just in case it doesn't work. To be successful, a spell requires the energy you are willing to give it and if there is any doubt or lack of faith in that energy then your spell is unlikely to be successful.

3. Cast your own spells – I recommended that you write and cast your own spells as it will allow for a much greater chance of success than if you are casting a

spell someone else wrote for you. However, you can cast spells written by other people but make sure they were not made for personal reasons otherwise the same results might not work for your specific needs. Also don't write a spell and ask someone else to cast it for you. You may think that this will make it more likely to be successful especially if you are only a beginner and the person who is offering to cast the spell for you is a professional, but this will not guarantee its success. Any true Wiccan or magickal practitioner will tell you that the best person to cast a spell for you is you.

4. Remember that a Wiccan harms none – You should NEVER cast a spell that will lead to an outcome that will bring harm or negative energy on someone else. You cannot cast a spell hoping to cause harm to someone or to go against someone's right to free will. There are many ways you can cast a spell that can bring harm to someone so you must be extremely careful when writing your own spells or the thoughts you have in mind at the time of the casting. This includes making someone fall in love with you with a love spell; it goes against their free will and will harm them. Obviously casting a spell wishing or hoping for revenge on another person goes against the Wiccan Rede.

5. The Rule of Three – When casting a spell, writing a spell, or taking part in any kind of magickal creation, The Rule of Three must be kept in mind at all times. This is for your own safety for as the rule states: any energy, whether it be negative or positive, that a Wiccan puts out into the world will be returned to them three fold / three times. So if you cast a spell wishing something to happen to someone else, you will invoke the Rule of Three and the same will

happen to you that is three times the magnitude of what you did. If you wish harm on someone then harm will return to you only it will be three times worse. If you wish something good for someone then the positivity will be returned to you in some way three times better than it was sent out. Keep this in mind when working with any form of magick.

6. The most important thing is You – You are the key ingredient to any spell, or magical creation, or even a ritual. It's your energy that the magick needs to get going, without your willingness to put your energy into your work then there would be no magick in what you are creating. So no matter how elaborate or simple the magick is, it is nothing without you.

## Casting a Spell

- Make sure you are well prepared:

A lot of preparation needs to be done before you can begin casting a spell. Without preparation you could get lost, forget what to do, stutter an incantation and then the spell will simply go wrong in all kinds of ways, or it just won't work. There are several things you can prioritize for preparation before you begin.

1. State your intent – you need to make sure you know what you want out of the spellcasting. The very reason you're performing a spell in the first place, it must be the first and last thing on your mind before, during and after the spell casting. Before beginning, you need to identify what you want, your need and what your gaol for the spell casting is.

It can be personal, so something you want to happen to your-self or someone close to you (with their permission only) to directly benefit from.

You don't need to be specific, not with all kinds of spells or magick, but it does help to narrow down the paths the spell has to take a little. If you want to wish for better luck and work or in your love life, that's fine, just a little too ambigu-ous. There are too many routes for the magick to take to get you what you asked for and it might lead to something you weren't entirely expecting or hoping for. So try to be as specific as possible.

Be simple, something that is complex or too intricate can only lead to disaster as it may be difficult to state everything you want in one small spell. It is best to break your ultimate goal down into smaller gaols and several spells that will eventu-ally lead you down the path you want to travel.

Finally don't be negative, be positive. Don't use negative words as this has a chance to put negative energy into the spell and change the outcome. For example, instead of incanting spells to stop the rain, instead try a spell to bring about sunshine.

1. Timing is everything – Don't leave timing to chance. Deciding on a random day early in the morning that you want to perform a spell that same night is a poor decision. It can be done, it's not as if the spell won't work correctly or you'll be doing something wrong, it's just not the best way to go about things. There are several days in which the air is abundant with natural magick which would guarantee your success in spellcasting as it will also heighten your own magickal energy. Such days as the Esbats, (13 full moons of the year) or the Sabbats, and many other

days. You can choose to plan your spellcasting around days like this but it isn't necessary.

2. Make a list – You'll need plenty of supplies if you're going to be casting a spell and it's a priority to make sure that you have all of that ready and waiting. You can't be in the middle of a spell casting, realize you don't have a crucial ingredient and either decide you don't actually need it, or run out and get it. This will disrupt the magickal energy and ruin the spell for good. So save yourself the trouble and check that list three times!

3. The Spell – This is obviously one of the most important things. You can't just find, or write a spell and decide it's good enough and use it. You have to be certain. In order to properly state your intent, you need to read, rewrite, edit, and analyse the spell until you're sure that it is as perfect as you could possibly make it. Although you don't have to memorize the incantation by heart, knowing it fairly well is important. Even if you're going to be reading from notes during the casting and not reciting it by heart, if you didn't give it a good look over beforehand then you are bound to stutter and make mistakes. This will, again, disrupt the magickal energy.

4. Prepare yourself and your space – Last but not least is the cleansing and preparation of both you and your sacred place (Altar). Clean the area and yourself in a purifying bath. Smudge the area if needed and make sure you are centered and calm. During the time leading up to the spell, you must make sure that you are comfortable within that space and that there is no chance of you being disturbed in the middle of the casting. This is possibly the most important step that must be taken before spell casting.

- Assess Your State of Mind

Making sure that your mind is in the right state is essential and you should begin this process during the very beginning of your preparation. You need to be focused on your intent and goals. If you want the magick to work, you need to believe in your conscious and unconscious mind that it will. Regular meditation is a good idea if you want to have a well-disciplined mind. Your mental state is important when it comes to spellcasting and any form of magickal creation.

During the time leading up to when you want to cast your spell, this can be days, weeks, or even months before, you must think positive. Your positive thoughts have more power than you could imagine and keeping that positive energy alive and building it up before the spell casting can help a tremendous amount. Having any kind of negative feelings or thoughts before casting the spell can have the opposite effect and ruin the spell completely. You can't be worrying about whether or not the spell is going to work or if you're going to make a mistake, you have to remain positive all the way through.

During the spell casting, you must keep your focus fixed on the spell and only the spell. What you are doing at that exact time is all that matters and nothing else. If your focus is broken and you start thinking about what you're going to do tomorrow or if you took the trash out this morning, then the magick will be interrupted. While casting the spell, all your energy and focus must be fixed on the task at hand and the ultimate goal of the spell. You must be able to see yourself reaching your hand out and grabbing hold of your intent. The spell must absorb your mind and you must allow it.

Once the spell is complete, your thoughts must remain as positive as they were before. If any sort of negative energy or doubt enters your mind then it could affect the results of the spell casting. You could start thinking about whether or not the magick will work and you could end up sabotaging yourself. If at all possible, it's best not to even think about the spell or the goal you set out for. However, this may be too difficult so if you are going to think about it then try your best to only think about it positively. Banish all doubt and worry and know that with the right energy you can achieve what you set out for.

- Create a Link

It's not enough to be focused on your goal during the spell casting; yes it helps but for the best results you should try and create a link between you and your goal. There are several ways to create a strong, unbreakable link to your goal and during the spell casting, you can even employ more than one at a time. Once there is a proper link established between you and your goal, there should be nothing to stop you from obtaining it.

1. State what your goal is – Shout it out from the roof tops and let the whole universe know what you want. Once you say it and hear it yourself then you make it a reality. You make it yours and the link begins to form.
2. Visualize it – If you can create the goal in your mind and see yourself taking it into your hands then a strong link will form. If you can visualize yourself obtaining your goal then what can stop you from doing so?
3. Power in Objects – When spell casting, it may be easier to create a link between yourself and your goal if it was represented by a solid object. Sometimes the visualization isn't enough and you might need something you can see right in front of you. Objects

you can touch with your bare hands. Personal items hold the most magickal energy and are the best objects to use in order to create a link to your goal. This is why some spells require ingredients like hair, nails, and sometimes blood, this is known as sympathetic magick and sometimes requires the use of a "Poppet" or a "Voodoo Doll."

Objects like candles can also be used to create a link, you can use the candle to represent your goal. Seeing the candle should make visualizing easier for you.

1. The five senses – Your senses are your best tools, use them to create the link you need. Sight, scent, touch, taste, sound; you can use any of these to represent your goal. For instance, if you wish for love and the smell of roses reminds you of love then surround yourself with roses during your spell casting. Or if you want wealth and the feel of a silky throw reminds you of that then wrap yourself in one during the spell casting.

- How to use the Energy properly

I would say that energy is the most important ingredient in any form of magick. Without your energy and the energy from the world around you, there would be no magick at all. Knowing how to use the energy within you and help it work alongside the energy around you is the secret key to being successful in your magick. There are different levels of energy and several steps that need to be taken during spell casting to ensure that the energy is being utilized properly.

Raising energy – Everything has energy, all of existence carries its own energy, and during your spell casting you will need to draw energy from the sources available to you. After creating the link to your goal, the next step is to raise energy. Some of this energy will come from inside of you; this is why your state of mind is so important. Being focused on your goal will help to direct your emotional, mental, and physical energy towards it.

Once you have directed your internal energy towards your goal then the rest of the energy you will need is going to come from outside sources. These sources can vary and you can use as many of them as you think you will need. These sources are the Moon, Sun, Earth, the Goddess and God or Elements, if you have invoked them, even the tools you have decided to use.

Raising energy will take a while as you must let it build up slowly. You must let the energy rise for as long as possible or until you feel it has reached its capacity. The more energy you raise, the more power it will have when you release it. The exact amount of time varies, some Wiccans feel that a few minutes are long enough and others prefer to wait for hours instead. You will need to practice this and experiment until you find the amount of time that works for you.

Methods for raising energy:

- Chanting
- Drumming
- Dancing
- Rocking back and forth

Direct the energy and release it – Once you have raised a sufficient amount of energy then it is time release it. Before you release the energy, you need to direct it, otherwise you might just release all that power out into a big world where it could end up anywhere, or nowhere.

To direct the energy, simply continue to do what you've been doing during the whole process. Focus on your goal; this is where you want the energy to go.

Once the energy has a direction it is ready to be released, this can be done in many ways and it depends on the type of magick you are preforming. If you are working with potions then drinking it releases the magick. Some Wiccans will burn something, shout, stomp their feet, or even break something to signify the spell is complete. You can also say something or gesture to seal the spell; throwing up your hands or bowing your head are traditional gestures.

As the last step, you will want to ground yourself to make sure there isn't any excess energy left inside you. You can visualize the energy pouring out of you into the earth or another object of significance.

A final tip to make sure your spells are successful is to create many paths for your magick to travel down. I mentioned earlier that when you cast a spell there are usually many pathways for the energy to take in order to get to the ultimate goal you wanted. These pathways do not appear by them-selves, you need to make them. Making paths for your magick is the difference between having success in spell casting and failure.

For instance, if you cast a spell for love, you can't spend all your time at home and expect the magick to drop the love of your life at your front door. You can't let the magickal energy do all of the work, you threw it out there and now you have to follow through and help it find its way. If you cast a spell for love, then go out to busy places on the weekend, join a dating site. Take the first step and your magick will follow through with the rest.

Even if you follow all the tips and tricks for a successful spell casting, it won't work if you don't make a path for your energy to travel down. It can make the path itself but it will take longer and you may not get the exact results you were hoping for.

## LIST OF SPELLS TO TRY

### Spells for Abundance and Wealth

Here are some prosperity spells to bring wealth and promote abundance in your life. Most of these spells will work as long as you aren't using them to be greedy. Most wealth and abundance spells won't work if you want the money but don't need it. All prosperity spells are associated with the element of Earth.

### Spice up your Wallet

This is a spell to bring you wealth and it is possibly the easiest spell to perform which makes it perfect for any beginners or newcomers to the Wiccan religion. The ingredients list for this spell is very short and you won't even need to perform a ritual of any kind. It's as easy as step 1, 2, 3;

Ingredients:

- Ground cinnamon
- Paper money (any amount, no coins)
- Your Wallet or purse (Wherever you keep your money)

Process:

This spell must be performed every Thursday to ensure its success, with any magick, practice makes perfect.

On Thursday, you must rub some cinnamon onto your finger tips and make 5 smudges on your paper money. Put the money into your wallet or purse and leave it there all week. This will attract new wealth as long as you repeat the process with the same money every Thursday.

It's as simple as that.

## Growing Wealth

This is also a simple spell and requires very few ingredients but if done correctly it will ensure the growth of wealth in your life.

Ingredients:

- A healthy houseplant (this can be any plant as long as it is healthy and thriving, however, a Basil plant would be the best option)
- Some dried patchouli
- A coin

Process:

Take your healthy houseplant and sprinkle a little bit of the patchouli on a small patch of soil. Then take the coin and stick it in the soil in the same place that you sprinkled the patchouli, make sure that some of the coin is still sticking out of the soil.

After the spell is complete, you must wait for the magickal energy to find its path. If it is a success and some new money appears in your life then you must spend the coin you've placed into the soil immediately and put a new one in its place.

## Candle Spell for Abundance

This spell isn't as simple as the others but it is still easy enough to perform and the flame from the burning candle will bring new financial opportunities your way.

Ingredients:

- Vanilla oil (extract if you can't get the oil)
- A large denomination coin
- Cinnamon oil
- A greed candle (used to represent wealth)

Process:

Use a sharp tool, (your ritual knife if you have one) to carve the word "Wealth" along the side of the green candle, then anoint (rub) the cinnamon and vanilla oil over the word. Place the denomination coin at the bottom of a candle holder then put the candle on top of it. Light the candle and let it burn all the way down.

Take the wax covered coin and keep it in a safe place and if the spell has been done correctly, you should expect it to bring money into your life.

Silver Spell

This spell will need to be performed on the night of a full moon and the skies must be clear so the light of the moon can shine into your work place.

Ingredients:

- One silver coin
- Seven Basil leaves (fresh)
- A cauldron or ceramic bowl
- Water (preferably rain or spring water)

Process:

The coin doesn't have to completely silver but it does need to have some silver in it and the ceramic bowl is a replacement for a cauldron but a cauldron is the best option.

Put the coin in the bottom of the cauldron or bowl and pour the water over it until the cauldron is about half full but that's up to you. Put the cauldron or bowl somewhere the moonlight can shine on it. Drop the Basil leaves into the water one at a time and speak this incantation clearly:

*By the light of the moon, bless me soon.*

*Water and silver shine, wealth be mine.*

Leave the cauldron or bowl there until the next morning then empty out the water and basil. Pour the water out into your garden or somewhere outside instead of down your drain, this way some of the excess energy can be returned to the earth.

Keep the coin with you in your pocket and it should bring wealth into your life in the near future.

Three Bells of Wealth

Bring some new money into your life with this easy wealth spell.

Ingredients:

- Pine oil
- A silver bell (any bell will work but a silver one is best)
- Three green candles (the green represents wealth)
- One silver or white candle (this candle represents you)

Process:

Anoint (rub) all four candles with the pine oil and place the three green candles in a triangular shape with the silver or white one in the centre. Put some of the pine oil on your hands as well. Now light the green candles and ring the bell three times, then say this incantation:

*Ring, ring, ring, the sound of bells.*

*Ring, ring, ring, the sound of wealth.*

Then light the silver candle in the centre, ring the bell three times again, and say:

*Ring, ring, ring, bring money to me.*

*Ring, ring, ring, by the power of three.*

Let all the candles burn down naturally. Leave the stubs and the bell on your altar until new money has entered your life. If you move them before then you may sabotage the spell.

## Money Chant

This is a chant to be spoken for financial access and to attract money in your future. You do not need any special ingredients for this spell but there are a few things you can do to ensure its success.

You can burn basil, or any other herb that is associated with prosperity and wealth. You can also light a green candle at your Altar during your chant. Small things like this can help with the success of your spell but they are by no means necessary for its success.

*Money, money, comes to me in abundance three times three.*

*May I be enriched in the best of ways, harming none of its way.*

*This I accept, so mote it be. Bring me money three times three.*

<u>Money-Doubling Spell</u>

This is an easy spell you can use to double any amount of money you use during the incantation. Remember as with all wealth and prosperity spells, you cannot be greedy. Do this only if you need it.

Ingredients:

- An amount of money (paper money is best)
- A white envelope
- A green candle

Process:

First you must take the amount of money you have and put them in a new envelope and seal it. Fold the envelope in half, making sure to fold it towards you, and chant this:

*Powers that be, to me shall bring the means to double this sum.*

*Hear me, you spirits that sing, quickly and gently come.*

You must do this once a day every day for seven days. You should hold the envelope in front of you as you chant and try envisioning it getting heavier. Keep the money in the envelope and somewhere safe when you are not performing a spell.

Once the spell has been complete and you have received the money you were asking for, you can spend or deposit the money that you've been keeping in the envelope. If you wish to cast the spell again, you must use a new batch of money.

**Spells for Health**

Spells for health and healing are very difficult to perform and are not always guaranteed success. Physical health is always tricky to influence, more than emotional or mental health but there are a few things you can do that can help your overall health.

Power of Three Healing Spell

There is strength in numbers and in the Wiccan religion, the numbers three and seven are the most powerful numbers. This spell utilizes the power of three to help speed up the healing of an illness. This is better for someone who is ill and will not work in the desired manner on someone with physical injuries. If you wish to perform this on yourself, make sure you are well enough to focus on the spell properly. You'll find that most health spells are more difficult to perform than others.

Ingredients:

- Three candles (one blue, one purple, and one white)
- Three pieces of quartz
- Three small pieces of paper
- Mint oil
- Sandalwood oil
- Myrrh oil

Take the three candles and anoint (rub) all of them with the mint, myrrh, and sandalwood oil. Place them in a triangular shape on your altar, making sure they are evenly apart from each other. Anoint (rub) the three quartz stones in the oils as well and then place one in front of each candle. Lastly, write the name of the person the healing spell is aimed at on each of the three pieces of paper and place them in the centre of the candles.

Light the candles and focus on the person that is ill that you wish to heal. Try to visualize them being healthy, picture them in your mind as strongly as you can while the candles burn. Say this three times:

*Magick mend and candle burn.*

*Illness leave and health return.*

You need to let the candles burn for precisely 3 hours. Blow them out and the spell is complete. If you want to add some extra power to your spell then repeat the ritual three nights in a row. The person this spell is aimed at should start to improve and the illness should fade.


## Lunar Healing

This spell must be done during a full moon and can only be done on you; it will not work on anyone else.

Ingredients:

- A long strip of white cloth
- A white candle
- A white flower blossom (any will do but it must be fresh)
- A safe place to perform the spell outdoors (you must not be disturbed)

Process:

You can perform this spell indoors if you have no other option but make sure you do it in front of a window with a clear view of the moon.

Light the candle and place it somewhere it isn't going to get knocked over. Let the moonlight wash over you and look up at it. Ask it to make you healthy while you focus on getting better and visualize yourself feeling healthy. Hold up the white flower and repeat this incantation softly but clearly:

*Moon Goddess, hear my call.*

*Please visit me in the moonlight.*

*Bless my body and my soul.*

Then gently wrap the strip of white cloth around your body where you want the healing energy to be directed. It's a symbolic act so it doesn't have to be perfectly wrapped around the area. Repeat the healing request again and stand in the moonlight for a little longer, a few minutes should be enough but you can stand there longer if you think it's necessary. Visualize the healing energy flowing over your body and healing your illness.

When you are finished, remove the cloth from your body and blow out the candle. Fold the cloth into a small bundle and keep it in a safe place in your room until you are healed.

Note: You don't have to use the Moon Goddess in the incantation if she isn't part of your beliefs. You can substitute the Moon Goddess for whatever deities in your belief represents the moon or if you don't worship any deities, you can simply ask the Moon itself to heal you.

Pentacle of Purification

This is a simple spell for simple healing. It won't work on illness or injury that is too serious. It works as a simple pick-me-up, or maybe if you have an unwanted headache.

Ingredients:

- A cup of water (preferably rain or spring water)
- A sprig of fresh rosemary

- Rose oil or Sandalwood oil

Process:

You will need to be topless to perform this spell so make sure you are alone and will not be disturbed.

Anoint (rub) the tip of the rosemary sprig with the oil you've chosen and use it to gently trace your chest or belly area in a pentacle shape. Touch the tip of the sprig to each of the points, and say "Earth, air, wind, fire, water, spirit" with each point.

While doing this try to picture the nature of the symbol and let it purify and cleanse your body. Take a drink of the water and bury the rosemary outside. This should cleanse your body of the illness.

Healing Hands Spell

This health spell is designed to target an injury on a specific part of your body. This will not work if you want to heal your whole body. You can use this spell for another person as well as for yourself.

Ingredients:

- Three candles (one pink, one lavender, one white)
- Vanilla oil

Light all the candles and place them on your altar, they don't need to be in a specific order. Take a little bit of the vanilla oil and use it to draw a circle with a dot in the centre of both your palms. You don't need a lot of the vanilla oil, just enough to trace on your palms.

Let your hands hover over the candles so you can feel their warmth, not close enough to burn yourself. Hold your hands over each of the candles and say:

*By this heat and light, with strength and might, I wish to heal my body.*

Feel the energy from the heat in your hands and then place them on the part of your body that you want to heal. Repeat the incantation above while you hold your hands in place. When you can no longer feel the added heat from the candles coming from your hands, the spell is complete.

You can blow the candles out and wash the oil off of yourself. You should start feeling better soon if the spell was successful.

Easy Health Blessing

This spell is a simple blessing and not a spell used to cure any illness or lessen any kind of pain. Its main use is to ensure a healthy future but this doesn't mean that if you jump off your roof that the spell will protect you. This blessing only prevents negative energy that wishes to harm you.

The ingredients you will use in this spell are used to represent health but do not have any actual medical abilities.

Ingredients:

- A cup of apple juice
- A stick of cinnamon
- A white candle

With most spells, the fresher and more natural the ingredients are the better it is for the success of the spell. If you can provide some fresh and natural ingredients, it is best but it is not necessary.

Pour the juice into a glass and stir it with the stick of cinnamon. Stir it four times then light the candle and drink a few sips of the juice. Say this incantation:

*May the Goddess bless this body and this soul.*

*Health and wellness is my goal.*

Drink the rest of the apple juice and blow out the candle. You can perform this spell whenever you feel an illness coming on or if you feel a little under the weather. You can also perform the spell early each morning just to make sure you keep in good shape.

Watch Your Step

This spell is for protection against negative energy out of your home and out of your life. This leads to a healthy lifestyle and productivity in healing spells.

Ingredients:

- One rusted screw or nail
- Three pieces of broken glass
- One clove of garlic

Process:

Note: Be very careful and exercise caution when dealing with the ingredients for this spell. Wear gloves and avoid the sharp edges of any of these objects.

Dig a hole that is preferably 6 inches deep outside your front door, and drop all the ingredients in making sure that the garlic is the last item added. Pour dirt back into the hole until it is properly covered and stand on top of the spot. Say this loud and clear:

*At this point, negativity stops*

Then leave the items in the ground to keep out negative energy and bad influences that wish to enter your home. The completion of this spell should bring you protection and promote a healthy lifestyle.

Abracadabra Health Spell

This spell is the simplest spell you can perform to bring health your way and heal yourself. This spell has been around since ancient times but it has been proven to work. You will need only three ingredients for this spell;

- A small piece of paper
- A pencil
- A piece of string to hang around your neck

Take the piece of paper and write the word "Abracadabra" on it, write a few lines but with each line write the word with one less letter:

ABRACADABRA

ABRACADABR

ABRACADAB

ABRACADA

ABRACAD

ABRACA

ABRAC

ABRA

ABR

AB

A

Now roll the paper up and use the string to wear the paper around your neck. You can use something else beside the string if you want.

The belief of this ancient spell is that the illness will disappear just like the word does.


**Spells for Happiness**

Happiness spells can help improve your mood and remove negative energy from your life, but remember that they can't replace real happiness. Make sure your heart is open to change when performing these spells; if you are determined to remain in a negative frame of mind, then no amount of magickal energy will help you. You have to be willing to lift your mood and the magickal energy will help you on your way there.

Happiness Candle Spell

This is a simple spell to help bring more positivity into your life. There are very few ingredients needed for this spell but it is still very effective.

Ingredients:

- Dried Lavender
- Two orange candles

Sprinkle a few pinches of the dried lavender on your Altar, or wherever your work place is, between the two candles. Light both the candles and hover your hands over the flames so you can feel the warmth. Repeat the following incantation precisely seven times:

*This spell please bless, for my happiness.*

Let the candles burn down naturally and the spell is complete. You should start to feel more joy in your life again in no time.

### Winds of Change Spell

This spell is mostly used to release stress and anger but that is only the first step to bringing more happiness into your life. You will need a special set of ingredients for this spell.

Ingredients:

- Basil
- Patchouli
- A hill
- A windy day

Process:

It's not necessary to perform the spell on a hill but an open area will be best for such a happiness spell like this one. The wind is mandatory; you can't perform the spell properly without it.

Go to your chosen spot, a hill or open area and face away from the wind so it is blowing against your back. Throw your herbs in the air and try to picture all your problems being blown away along with the herbs. Say the following incantation:

*May the winds of change take my pain and make me happy once again.*

Turn around to face the wind and say;

*May the winds bring joy to me so that happy I will be.*

Stand there for a few moments, feeling the wind on your face and focusing on releasing all your stress and anger. Feel a sense of peace and acceptance fill your body.


Blossoms of Happiness

This spell is simple and one of the best ways to bring positive energy back into your life.

Ingredients:

- A yellow candle
- Paper
- Pencil
- Jasmine oil or Lilac oil
- One fresh flower (any flower is fine but try to pick one that corresponds with happiness and joy)
- A bowl

Process:

Light the yellow candle and then write 3 things that are in your life that make you unhappy on the piece of paper. Touch the flames with the paper, drop it in the bowl and let it burn.

Rub the flower with your chosen oil and make sure to breathe the spell in deeply. Visualize your stress, anger, and all your problems disappearing as the paper turns to ash. Place the flower in the bowl on top of the ash to replace all the negative energy with joy. You can leave the bowl on your Altar as a reminder to be happy.

. . .

## Three Candles for Joy

This spell will bring that little bit of joy and happiness into your life when you need it the most.

Ingredients:

- Three yellow or orange candles
- Rosemary
- Marjoram
- Cedar oil

Process:

Anoint (rub) all three candles with the oil and place them on your Altar. Light the candles then sprinkle the herbs on each on the table surrounding the candles. Focus on the heat coming from the flames and repeat this incantation:

*Happiness and joy, come into my life*

*Away with anger, stress, and strife*

*I am happy and I am free*

*No more negativity*

Hover your hands over the flames and feel their warmth, but be careful not to burn or hurt yourself. Focus on the positive energy in your life and feel the determination fill you as you leave the candles to burn down naturally.

## A Hushed Moment Spell

You can use this spell to bring some peace into your life if you are feeling stressed or if things are getting hectic. It is a simple spell and peace is only a single step on the way to happiness and joy.

Ingredients:

- One white feather
- A piece of white thread that is a few inches long

Process:

You need to be in a quiet place where you're sure you won't be disturbed in order to perform this spell. Tie one end of the thread to the feather and hold the other end between your forefinger and your thumb.

Let the feather dangle in front of your face. Blow on it gently and watch it swing around until it hangs still again. As you watch it swing back and forth, whisper these words:

*Still, quiet, hush*

*I'm not in a rush*

When the feather is still once again, repeat the incantation one more time and the spell is complete.


## Rid Yourself of Negative Energy Chant

This is not a spell but a chant and does not require any special ingredients or circumstances to be performed. However, it could help if you close yourself in a safe place where you feel relaxed and comfortable and you are sure you will not be disturbed.

Once you are safe, relaxed, and in a comfortable state of body and mind, repeat the following incantation:

*I see only pure reflected light*

*I am ridding myself of all bad luck*

*I am ridding myself of all negativity*

*O Blessed Be*

While you speak the incantation, close your eyes and breathe deeply and calmly. Try to imagine a white, warm light glowing around you coming from inside. This should rid you of all negative energy in your life and bring you new joy and happiness.

### Know the Child Within

This is a simple spell, or ritual, that does not require too many ingredients. If this spell is done correctly, it should reconnect you to your inner child. This should bring about a natural joy and happiness that only children can feel.

Ingredients:

- A doll or stuffed animal (an old one from your childhood would be best but any will work)
- Some salt water
- One blue or green candle
- A piece of white cloth

Process:

You need to begin by casting a ritual circle around your Altar. You must sit at your Altar making sure to face south and light the candle. Take the doll or stuffed animal in your hands and sprinkle it with the salt water.

Say:

*I name you (use you a nickname or any special name given to you in your childhood).*

You want to put enough of your magickal energy into the doll or stuffed animal until it can represent you. Hold it in your arms as you rock it back and forth and speak to it. Tell it something you would have wanted someone to tell you when you were a child. Treat it the way you wanted to be treated as a child. Let it talk back to you and tell you what it wants and how it's feeling. Play with it, let your voice change into that of a younger more carefree version of yourself.

Raise the magickal energy inside of you as you visualize it pouring out of you and into the doll of a stuffed animal. Continue raising the energy and pouring it into the toy until you can visualize it glowing with white light and warm love.

Kiss the doll or stuffed animal to seal the spell then gently wrap it up in the white cloth. Leave the doll or stuffed animal to rest at your Altar. To complete the spell or ritual, simply ground yourself and open the circle.

You should feel more carefree and joyous as you rekindle the connection to the child within you. You can repeat this spell as often as you need or want to.


**Spells for Love and Relationships**

There are many forms of love so there are of course just as many forms of love spells. If you want to bring your ex-partner back your way or if you want to bring a new love into your life, then that requires an "attraction spell." If you are leaning towards having a long term, committed relationship then "true love spells" work the best. Or if you're looking for someone that is willing to go all the way with you then a "marriage spell" is the best way to go.

With any kind of love spell, it's important to remember that you cannot force someone to love you. This will be going against their free will and the Wiccan Rede.


Ring a Bell Love Spell

This spell is once again simple with very few ingredients but sure to be successful in finding you that love you're looking for.

Ingredients:

- A silver bell (silver is the best choice but it's not necessary)
- A piece of paper

Write a small note on the piece of paper that lists all of the qualities that you want in your new love. Read them out aloud and clearly, and then ring the bell. Fold the paper up until it is small enough to fit underneath the bell and set the bell down on top of it.

Repeat this process each day for four days; remove the note, read it out loud and place it back under the bell. After the fourth day, leave the bell and paper at your Altar until you find your new love.

Fair Feathers Touch

Love is often associated with the element air and a feather is one of the best ways to represent that element. This simple spell is a great way to bring new love into your life.

Ingredients:

- A feather (any size or color is fine as long as it is real)
- A Pink ribbon
- A sprig of rosemary (dried out preferably)

Process:

Take the ribbon and use it to tie the sprig of rosemary to the feather, creating a love charm. Hang the charm on the inside of your bedroom door handle. Make sure to touch the charm every time you leave or enter your bedroom and a new love will find its way to you.

## Love Drawing Spell

This is a quick and simple spell to perform although it is more of an attraction spell than it is a love spell. It won't get anyone to love you but it will draw their attention towards you and then you can take it from there.

Ingredients:

- A photo of a rose
- A red marker
- An envelope
- A stamp for the envelope

Process:

Take a picture of the rose and, using the red marker, write the name of the person you wish to attract to you. Make sure you write their name in big letters. If you don't have a name of someone specific and simply want a new love in your life then just write the words "my ideal partner" on it instead.

Fold up the picture and place it in the envelope, place the stamp on it, address it to yourself, and then mail it. The further out you can send it the better as it will spread the attraction energy far and wide.

When the letter returns to you, keep it in your bedroom, without opening it, until you see some attention being directed your way.

## Bell of Beauty

This spell's really a beauty spell. It's a spell used to make you more attractive to that certain person whose interest you wish to attract. It can also be used to attract the attention of any one if you wish. This spell works best if a person is meant to be with you, so if someone other than the person your spell was directed at starts paying attention, then you know why.

Ingredients:

- Vanilla oil or extract
- A silver bell
- A handful of rose petals
- Pink, white, and red ribbon
- A shallow dish or saucer

Process:

Fill the dish or saucer with the rose petals, they can be fresh or dry, and tie all three ribbons to the handle of the bell. Repeat one line of this incantation with each ribbon you tie:

*The peal of the bell, the sound of the tone*

*It's about time our love has grown*

*Open (your target's name) eyes to see me alone*

Using your finger, rub the vanilla oil or extract along the rim of the bell. Repeat the incantation again and ring the bell with each line. Place the bell in the dish of petals and leave it on your Altar. Ring the bell in the morning when you wake up to activate the spell for that day. Your intended love interest will start to notice you soon or a person you are meant to be with may start to notice you instead.

Fire in Stone

This is not really a love spell but more of a passion spell. It's not very useful for attracting a new love to you but it is often used to ignite a new passion between you and your current lover.

Ingredients:

- One piece of Garnet
- One piece of Red Jasper
- One piece of Carnelian
- A glass or ceramic dish
- A red candle

Process:

Take any one of the three stones, hold it tightly in your hands and whisper the words;

*Love in fire, love in stone*

Place the stone in the glass or ceramic dish and then do the same thing to the other two stones. Now light your red candle and hover it over the dish at an angle. Keep it there so that the candle burns, melting the wax and letting it drip onto each stone equally. While the wax is dripping down onto the stones, say:

*Love to me, crystals three*

Keep the candle burning and the wax dripping until the stones are covered in a single layer of wax that connects them to one another. Draw a heart shape on the stones with a ritual tool or a sharp object while the wax is still wet.

You must let the candle burn out naturally at your Altar and leave the wax-covered stones there for about a week.

Compass of Love

A spell like this is not really used for finding a new love or getting back with an ex who no longer feels attraction to you. This spell is used to try and find a love that you've lost, say if the person you love has moved far away and you've lost touch with them. This spell can't make someone who doesn't love you anymore suddenly find their way back to you, I'm afraid love doesn't work that way. However, if you are looking to rekindle that long lost love then this spell may just work for you.

Ingredients:

- A compass
- Some rose petals (fresh)
- Dried rosemary
- A piece of Hematite or a piece of Lodestone
- A small square of white silk

Process:

Make sure you have a true traditional compass when performing this spell, a GPS or some sort of app won't work the right way.

Place the compass on your Altar or workplace and use it to find west. Stand facing west, leaving your compass on your Altar, and say:

*North, south, east, and west*

*Find for me who I love best*

*Where they've gone, I do not know*

*Bring me signs, I need them so*

Take the rosemary and sprinkle it in a circle around the compass, do the same with the rose petals. Cover the whole thing with the white silk and place the stone on top of the compass. Repeat the incantation again.

Leave the ingredients on your Altar for 3 days, some signs should start to appear to you, telling you where you can find your lost love. The compass is just a symbolic object; it won't actually point you in the right direction. There will be other signs that will do that.

### The Perfect Partner Candle Spell

This spell can be used to bring a specific person to you but it works better if you simply allow the universe to bring the perfect person to you. So try to avoid using names with this spell and the universe will provide the perfect partner you seek.

Ingredients:

- Some pink chalk
- Pink cloth or red cloth
- One candle of your favourite color
- One white candle
- A candle holder for each candle

Process:

This spell will take several days for it to work so you'll need to utilize your Altar or create a workspace.

Hold the white candle up in your hand and think about the qualities you want in a partner. Try to visualize them and try to not be too specific. You want something extremely unique or specific in your partner, like one blue eye and one green eye, then the magickal energy will have very few paths to travel down on the way to your goal and it might not get there at all. With all love spells, it's best not to be specific at all.

When you've finished visualizing the qualities you want in your partner, say them out loud while still holding onto the white candle and focusing your energy on it. It will now represent your future perfect partner. Take the candle in your favourite color and think of all the qualities that you will bring to this new relationship and say them out loud, focusing your energy on the candle. This candle now represents you.

Place the candles in their holders and lay the pink cloth out on your Altar. Set the candle holders down on the pink cloth about two feet from each other. Between the candles and in the centre of the cloth, use the chalk to draw a large heart.

Each evening you need to focus on the candles and visualize the relationship you are looking and hoping for. Each evening you will need to move the candles a little closer to one another. Do this until the candles are in the centre of the heart together but don't rush the process. Don't move the candles forward in leaps simply because you are growing impatient. Take your time and you will be rewarded. The exact amount of days depends on how you place the candles each night but the usual time is normally a week at the least.

When the candles are side-by-side in the heart you've drawn with the chalk, then the heart of the spell can begin. Take the chalk and draw a second bigger heart around the first one you drew. Ask your preferred Goddess of love to grant you your request for the perfect partner you've asked for to find their way to you. Light the candles and focus your energy on them for a short moment each evening.

Leave this set up on your Altar and re-light the candles again each evening, repeating the above process. Let the candles burn for as long as you can until they both burn down naturally. This is where the spell requires some patience from you as this part will take some time to complete.

Once the candles burn down naturally then the spell is complete. It shouldn't be long for your perfect partner to find their way to you or for you to find your way to them.

# AFTERWORD

So as you go forth on your path to the divine, remember the things you have learned along the way and do not hesitate to teach them yourself. The greatest gift a Wiccan can give is to pass on the knowledge they have obtained so that the religion and tradition can continue to grow and prosper.

Do not judge others who would judge you, not everyone sees the ways of Wicca the same way we do. They will find their path to the divine even if it is not the same path you take to get there. No path is the wrong path.

As long as it harms none, do what you will.

*Vivienne Grant*

# CHAPTER 11
# BIBLIOGRAPHY

1: Reference for Wiccan Origin and History

http://wiccaliving.com/history-of-wicca/

2: Reference for the different forms of Wiccan beliefs and traditions

http://wiccaliving.com/wiccan-traditions-wicca-forms/

3: Reference for the Oak king and Holly king

http://wiccaliving.com/wiccan-oak-king-holly-king/

4: Reference for the Rule of Three

https://en.m.wikipedia.org/wiki/Rule_of_Three_(Wicca)

5: Reference for the Wiccan Rede

https://www.thoughtco.com/the-wiccan-rede-2562601

6: Reference for Wiccan Philosophy

https://www.free-witchcraft-spells.com/wiccan-philosophy.html

7: Reference for Sabbats and Esbats

https://www.free-witchcraft-spells.com/pagan-holidays.html

8: Reference for Creating Your Altar

https://www.free-witchcraft-spells.com/pagan-altar.html

9: Reference for Your Book of Shadows

https://www.free-witchcraft-spells.com/book-of-shadows.html

10: First Reference for Herbs: A history

https://wicca.com/celtic/herbal/history.htm

11: Second Reference for Herbs: A history

http://wiccaliving.com/beginners-guide-herbal-magic/

12: Reference for Wiccan Rituals

http://wiccaliving.com/wiccan-rituals/

13: Reference for Love spells

https://www.free-witchcraft-spells.com/free-easy-love-spells.html

14: First Reference for Health spells

https://www.free-witchcraft-spells.com/easy-magic-spells.html

15: Second Reference for Health spells

https://www.free-witchcraft-spells.com/protection-spells.html

16: Third Reference for Health spells

https://www.free-witchcraft-spells.com/healing-spells.html

17: Reference for Abundance and wealth spells

https://www.free-witchcraft-spells.com/free-money-spells.html

18: First Reference for Happiness spells

https://www.free-witchcraft-spells.com/easy-magic-spells.html

19: Second Reference for Happiness spells

https://www.free-witchcraft-spells.com/happiness-spells.html

20: Reference for Brews and Teas

https://witchesofthecraft.com/category/brews-and-teas/

21: Reference for Oils

http://blessedbe.sugarbane.com/oilrecipes.htm

22: First Reference for Charms

https://witchofhowlingcreek.wordpress.com/2013/02/19/the-a-z-guide-to-charm-bags-part-1/

23: Second Reference for Charms

https://www.free-witchcraft-spells.com/fortune-spells.html

24: Third Reference for Charms

https://www.free-witchcraft-spells.com/spells-for-love.html

25: First Reference for Magickal Herbs

https://www.thoughtco.com/magical-herbs-to-have-on-hand-2562042

26: Reference for Dangerous herbs

https://www.thoughtco.com/toxic-and-poisonous-herbs-2562022

Made in the USA
Monee, IL
17 October 2023

44777506R00077